English G 21

Klassenarbeitstrainer
für Schülerinnen und Schüler

mit Lösungen und Lerntipps

Vokabel Trainer
Cornelsen

Vokabeltrainer-App

Verfügbar für: iOS, Android und Windows Phone

Cornelsen

English G 21 • Band A 3

Klassenarbeitstrainer mit Lösungen und Lerntipps

Konzeption
Dr. Ursula Mulla und Nogi Mulla, Germering

Erarbeitet von
Bärbel Schweitzer M.A., Staufen
Senta Friedrich, Tamm
Timo Keller, Kornwestheim

In Zusammenarbeit mit der Englischredaktion
Dr. Christiane Kallenbach (Projektleitung)
Stefanie Bayer (verantwortliche Redakteurin)
Susanne Bennetreu, Ulrike Berendt (Bildredaktion)

Beratende Mitwirkung
Angela Ringel-Eichinger, Bietigheim-Bissingen

Illustrationen
Constanze Schargan, Berlin
Roland Beier, Berlin (S. 6, S. 29, S. 45/4)

Bildquellen
Alamy, Abingdon (S. 29, Bild 7: David Lyons); Britain on View, London (S. 29 Bild 1: Joe Cornish); Corbis, Düsseldorf (S. 12, Bild 3: Norbert Schaefer; S. 62: Tom Stewart; S. 63 li.: Stefanie Grewel / zefa / Corbis); blickwinkel, Witten (S. 12 Bild 4: F. Hecker); furryface (S. 10 unten); Getty, München (S. 29 Bild 3: Tim Graham; S. 32 oben re.: Rana Faure); istockphoto, Calgary (S. 10 rechts: Renars Jurovskis; S. 16 Tower Bridge: Junghee Choi, S. 19 unten re.: Jane Norton; S. 28: Monique Rodriguez; S. 52 Bild 1: dawn liljenquist, Bild 2: Katherine Moffitt, Bild 3: Rich Legg, Bild 4: Andreas Reh; S. 63 oben re.: Aleksej Vasic, unten re.: Tony Tremblay; S. 70: Jasmin Awad); The Lowry, Salford Quays (S. 41 li.); The LS Lowry Collection, Salford (S. 41 re.); Picture Alliance, Frankfurt / Main (S. 12 Bild 5: Jens Wolf); www.pitlochry.org.uk (S. 30 (Stand 15.06.09)); Shutterstock, New York (S. 8 girl: Edyta Pawlowska, boy: Joellen L. Armstrong; S. 9: Tracey Whiteside; S. 12 Bild 1: Nikolay Titov, Bild 2: Ragne Kabanova, Bild 6: Tatjana Strelkova; S. 16 London Eye: Brian A. Jackson, Big Ben: Edyta Pawlowska, Buckingham Palace: Mark William Richardson, hotel: Wendy Nero; S.19 oben re.: Felix Mizioznikov, unten li.: Gorilla, oben li.: Rui Vale de Sousa; S. 29 Bild 2: Stephen Finn, Bild 4: Kenneth William Caleno, Bild 6: Lance Bellers; S. 31: Four Oaks; S. 32 oben li.: Losevsky Pavel, unten li.: Orange Line Media, unten re.: robert paul van beets; S. 52 Bild 1: Jaimie Duplass; S. 58 tennis: JJ pixs, basketball: Orange Line Media, soccer: Robert J. Beyers II, jumping: Suzanne Tucker; S. 76: sint; S. 77: Ivan Montero Martinez)

Textquellen
S. 30: Tickets for Pitlochry Festival Theatre. Adapted from www.pitlochry.org.uk (Stand 15.06.09)
S. 47: AvH. Adapted from www.avh.montreal.qc.ac (Stand 15.06.09)
Lösungen S. 14: Auszug der Seiten 200, 589, 590 aus „English G 2000 Wörterbuch – Das Wörterbuch zum Lehrwerk". Herausgegeben von der Langenscheidt-Redaktion Wörterbücher und der Cornelsen-Redaktion Englisch. © 2002 Cornelsen Verlag GmbH & Co. OHG, Berlin und Langenscheidt KG, Berlin und München.

Titelbild
Constanze Schargan, Berlin; IFA-Bilderteam, Ottobrunn (Hintergrund Union Jack: Jon Arnold Images)

Layout und technische Umsetzung
Heike Freund, Hameln

Umschlaggestaltung
Klein und Halm Grafikdesign, Berlin

www.cornelsen.de
www.EnglishG.de

1. Auflage, 11. Druck 2017

Druck: H. Heenemann, Berlin

ISBN 978-3-06-032158-2

PEFC
PEFC/04-31-1156

PEFC zertifiziert
Dieses Produkt stammt aus nachhaltig bewirtschafteten Wäldern und kontrollierten Quellen.
www.pefc.de

INHALT

DIE NÄCHSTE KLASSENARBEIT KOMMT BESTIMMT …

Liebe Schülerin, lieber Schüler,
wer gut vorbereitet in eine Klassenarbeit geht, kann die Aufgaben in Ruhe und mit Konzentration bearbeiten und wird dann auch gute Ergebnisse erzielen. Der Klassenarbeitstrainer hilft dir dabei.
Du findest zu jeder Unit zwei Klassenarbeiten, mit denen du alle Fertigkeiten (skills) trainieren kannst, die du für die Klassenarbeiten benötigst.

Unsere Tipps für ein erfolgreiches Lernen mit deinem Klassenarbeitstrainer:

Vorbereitung
Mache dir vor der Klassenarbeit rechtzeitig einen Lernplan, in dem du festlegst, was du an welchem Tag bearbeiten willst. Plane dazu genügend Zeit ein. Hole dir bei Unklarheiten Hilfe. Am Tag vor der Arbeit wiederholst du nur kurz.

Lernheft
Besorge dir ein Schreibheft. Es dient für Schreibaufgaben und zusätzliche Übungen. Schreibe schön und übersichtlich (mit Datum, Überschrift, Aufgabe und Seite). Lege auf der 1. Seite ein Inhaltsverzeichnis an. So kannst du bei Unklarheiten immer wieder nachschlagen. Es hilft dir auch, wenn du eine Aufgabe ein zweites oder drittes Mal machen möchtest.

Lösungen
Du findest die Lösungen zusammen mit deinen Audios unter www.scook.de. Dort kannst du sie dir mit deinem Code freischalten. Dein Code steht am Anfang des Hefts auf der ersten Seite. Vergleiche deine Lösungen mit den Musterlösungen. Sieh dir dabei deine Fehler ganz genau an und überlege, was du falsch gemacht hast. Nur so kannst du daraus lernen und die Fehler in Zukunft vermeiden. In den Lösungen findest du auch die Hörtexte und Lerntipps mit weiteren Übungen.

Wiederholung
Aufgaben, die dir noch schwer fallen, solltest du ein zweites oder drittes Mal machen. Lass etwas Zeit zwischen den Wiederholungen verstreichen.

Punkteschlüssel
Er hilft dir, deine Leistung einzuschätzen.

Übrigens: Die Klassenarbeiten in diesem Heft prüfen das Gelernte sehr ausführlich ab. Du brauchst daher für die Bearbeitung länger als eine Schulstunde. Natürlich kannst du dir die Klassenarbeiten auch auf einzelne Tage aufteilen oder bestimmte Aufgaben ganz gezielt üben.

Let's get started!

Ich wünsche dir viel Erfolg und vor allem viel Freude beim Üben und Lernen mit deinem Klassenarbeitstrainer.

Have fun with English!

Bärbel Schweitzer

Gesamtpunktzahl 64,5 /74 Note 2

LISTENING

14 /15

01/02 Going to London

You're on holiday in Britain and listening to Radio Rainbow. It's the afternoon programme and the reporter is talking about a quiz on last week's show and is going to announce the winner.

About the radio show

6 /6

a) *Listen to the two texts and tick (✔) the correct box.*

		Right	Wrong
1	There was a quiz on the radio show.	✓	
2	Last week's radio show was about planning a trip to London.	✓	
3	You had to write a report about London to win a prize.		✓
4	Every listener had the right answer.		✓
5	The prize was a ticket for a music festival.		✓
6	You can win something in next week's show.	✓	

b) *Now listen to each of the texts again for details.*

Mache dir vor dem Hören bewusst, welche Einzelheiten du heraushören sollst. Lass dich nicht von anderen Einzelheiten ablenken.

01 Text 1

3 /3

Circle the correct information.

1 Victoria Park was opened in **1854 / 1845 / 1945**.

2 Chris answered the questions **in an e-mail / on the phone / in a letter**.

3 Chris **is a student / is too young for a trip to London / is from London**. →

02 Text 2

5 /6

The reporter talks to Tom about …
*Tick (✔) **Yes** or **No**.*

	Yes	No
1 … the dinner on the first evening.	✓	
2 … planning the sightseeing tour.		✓
3 … shopping in London.		✓
4 … a boat trip on the River Thames.	✓	
5 … free tickets for the theatre.		✓
6 … how Chris will travel to London.	✓	

x

LANGUAGE

35,5 /39

1 WORDS A quiz about transport

5 /8

Fill in the correct words.

1 If you want to fly to Australia, you must go to the a i r p o r t.
2 Your plane leaves from g a t e number B34.
3 If you need a ticket for the bus, you can get it from the ticket m a c h i n e.
4 Another word for the underground in London is the t u b e.
5 Let's see which p l a t f o r m the train leaves from.
6 A day ticket for the London underground is called a t r a v e l c a r d.
7 The colours on the Tube map show you the different l i n e s.
8 If you put the letters from the blue boxes in the right order, you get a verb that has to do with transport:

c h a n g e

a nech

2 WORDS Word groups

10 /10

*Find **five** more words for each word group.*

Instruments	Buildings and places in town
 fiddle	 cathedral
r ecorder	s quare
t rumpet	c ircus
f lute	l ane
c larinet	p alace
s axophone	b orough

3 GRAMMAR Before the weekend in London

5 /5

*It's Thursday evening, the evening before Chris and his father leave for their weekend in London. Write down what Chris and his father have already done and what they haven't done. Use **already** and **not ... yet** in your sentences.*

1

Chris and his father – pack – suitcases

2

Chris's father check – train times

3
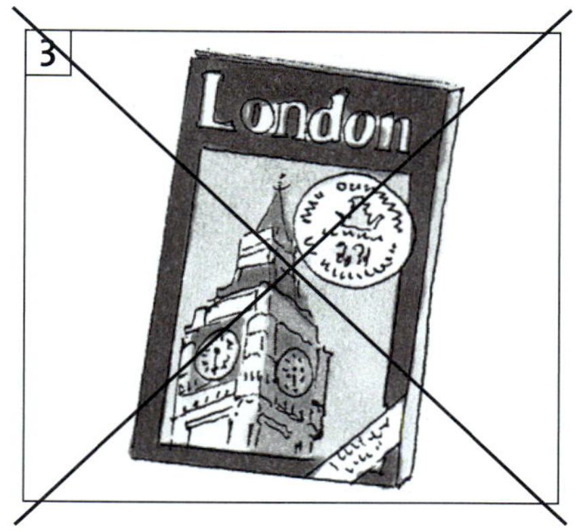

Chris – read – book about London

4

Chris's father – phone – hotel in London

5
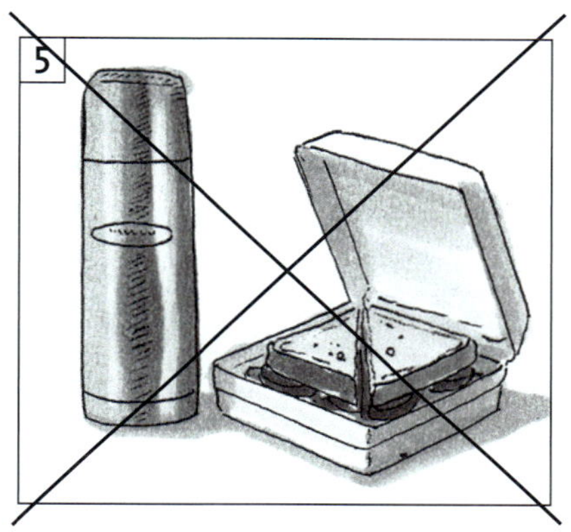
they – make – sandwiches for the train journey

1 Chris and his father have already packed their suitcases ✓
2 Chris's father has already checked the train times ✓
3 Chris hasn't read the book about London yet ✓
4 Chris's father has already phoned the hotel in London ✓
5 They haven't made sandwiches for the train journey yet. ✓

present perfect

Bildung:

I/you/we/they (Lisa and Ben) **have/haven't** open**ed** the window.
he (Ben, my father) / **she** (Lisa, my daughter) / **it** (the wind) **has/hasn't** open**ed** the window.

Verwendung:

Mit dem **present perfect** drückst du aus, dass etwas irgendwann in der Vergangenheit stattgefunden hat. Der genaue Zeitpunkt des Geschehens ist nicht wichtig oder nicht bekannt. Deshalb findest du oft Adverbien der unbestimmten Zeit:

I have **already** packed[1] my suitcase. (**already** steht vor dem past participle)
They haven**'t** read the book **yet**. (**yet** steht am Satzende)

[1] suitcase ['su:tkeɪs] *Koffer*

4 GRAMMAR Chris's guide book about London

4 /4

a) This is some information Chris has found in his guide book. Fill in the gaps with ***since*** *or* ***for****.*

1 London buses have been red for a long time.

2 Since March 2000 more than two million visitors have enjoyed a ride on the London Eye.

3 Tourists haven't been allowed to feed the pigeons[1] at Trafalgar Square for the last few years.

4 Lots of tourists have walked over the Millennium Bridge since it was opened in 2002.

present perfect mit *since* und *for*
Wenn du über einen Zustand sprichst, der in der Vergangenheit begonnen hat und bis jetzt andauert, verwendest du das **present perfect**:
since mit Zeitpunkten (last week, 2005, yesterday) ● ⟶ |
for mit Zeitspannen (two months, many years, a long time). | ⌒

5 GRAMMAR Chris in Hyde Park

11,5 / 12

On his last day in London, Chris spends some time in Hyde Park. There he talks to Janet, a teenage girl from London. Write their questions and answers. Use the present perfect with ***since*** *and* ***for****.*

1 be in London?
2 1998
3 be in Hyde Park?
4 have this funny T-shirt?
5 know about Hyde Park?
6 I read a book about Hyde Park

1 two days
2 live in London?
3 three hours
4 Sunday morning
5 a long time
6 be interested in parks?

1 ***Janet*** How long have you been in London? ✓

Chris I've already here for two days. ✓

2 ***Chris*** How long have you lived in London? ✓

Janet I've lived in London since 1998. ✓

3 ***Janet*** How long have you been in Hyde park? ✓

Chris I've been in Hyde Park for three hours. ✓

4 ***Janet*** How long have you had this funny t-shirt? ✓

Chris I've had the "funny" t-shirt since Sunday morning ✓

5 ***Janet*** How long have you known about the Hyde Park? 0,5

Chris I've knewn about the Hyde Park for a long time. ✓

6 ***Chris*** How long have you been interested in parks? ✓

Janet I've been interested in parks since I read a book about Hyde Park. ✓

[1] pigeon ['pɪdʒɪn] *Taube*

WRITING

15 / 20

A diary about our trip to London

In her summer holidays, Sue spends four days in London with her parents and her brother.
You are Sue and write your diary about your first day.
Write down what you liked ☺ and what you didn't like ☹. Write about your feelings[1] too. Write about 100 words.

☞ **Writing better sentences:**

Choose from these lists:

Linking words	**Adjectives**	**Adverbs**
Time phrases: at 7 o'clock, in the afternoon, then, next, at first, for an hour, after two hours, ... **Achtung:** Satzstellung bleibt: S-V-O: In the afternoon I played football. **Nicht:** ~~In the afternoon played I football.~~ Konjunktionen: although, and, because, but, ...	boring excited long angry happy nice spicy mild special great ...	very really ...

2 didn't find the hotel – Mum angry with Dad – no map of London ☹ (4P)

3 hotel super – rooms very nice – everybody happy ☺ (3P)

1 journey[2] to London by car – too long in the car!! ☹ (4P)

4 afternoon: first Buckingham Palace – boring ☹ – Hyde Park – relax ☺ (5P)

5 evening: Indian restaurant – food great ☺ – now tired (4P)

Start like this:

Dear diary,
Mum, Dad, Ron and I started our journey to London this morning ...

[1] feeling ['fi:lɪŋ] *Gefühl* [2] journey ['dʒɜ:ni] *Reise, Fahrt*

Klassenarbeit B

Gesamtpunktzahl ohne Speaking ______ / 65	Note ______
Gesamtpunktzahl mit Speaking ______ / 77	Note ______

READING

11,5 / 15

Victoria Park

London is famous for its parks: everybody knows Hyde Park and Regent's Park. Every day many people spend some time in one of the London parks. One of London's best kept secrets[1] is another park, Victoria Park. It is in the north-east of London and it is free. It's a fantastic place to spend some free time.

Queen Victoria opened the park in 1845 because more than 30,000 people asked for a park in the part of London called the East End. Of course Hyde Park is much older, but Victoria Park was the first park in the East End. In the park people could spend some time in the fresh air, see a lot of different trees and go for a walk with their children.

In the Victorian Age[2] everybody called it the "People's Park". One of the reasons for this name was that it was a park especially for working-class[3] people. People in the Victorian Age thought that parks helped working-class people to stay healthy and to live longer. Many children visited the park every day and for some children in the 1880s it was the only place with trees and grass where they could play. People could swim in the lakes too.

Today Grove Road runs through the park and so there are two parts, a smaller western part and an eastern part. You find a lot of attractions in the park: lakes where you can paddle, some exciting playgrounds, you can play cricket and football and see deer and goats. There is something interesting for everybody in the family.

Victoria Park is also famous for open-air music festivals. Every year in August there is the *Underage Festival* in Victoria Park. This event presents some of the best reggae, rock and electronic music for young music fans. The festival is for kids from 14 to 18 only, and no adults[4] are allowed. And it's a festival without alcohol. You may only drink juice, water and other non-alcoholic drinks. BBC 1 is a partner of this festival and records the live music for their radio programmes.

[1] secret ['siːkrət] *Geheimnis* [2] Victorian Age [vɪk'tɔːriən ˌeɪdʒ] *im Zeitalter von Königin Victoria (1837–1901)*
[3] working class *Arbeiterschicht* [4] adult ['ædʌlt] *Erwachsene(r)*

1 About Victoria Park

/3

Tick (✔) the three pictures that the text is about.

2 Victoria Park now and then

/12

Tick (✔) the correct boxes.

☞ Markiere in den Aussagen **Schlüsselwörter (key words)**, nach denen du im Text suchen kannst, um die gesuchte Information zu finden.

	Right	Wrong	Not in the text
1 Somebody from the Royal Family opened the park.			
2 In 1845 more than 30,000 people wanted a park in the north-east of London.			
3 Victoria Park is the oldest park in London.			
4 Another name for Victoria Park was the "People's Park" because many people visited the park every day.			
5 You can still swim in the lakes in Victoria Park today.			
6 Today there is a western part and a larger eastern part.			
7 You can watch animals in Victoria Park.			
8 Victoria Park is only interesting for children.			
9 You can only visit Victoria Park during[1] the day.			
10 You are not allowed to ride your bike in the park.			
11 You are not allowed to drink alcohol at the *Underage Festival*.			
12 You can listen to some of the music from the *Underage Festival* on the radio.			

[1] during ['dʒʊərɪŋ] *während*

LANGUAGE

1 /40

1 GRAMMAR Wednesday afternoon at Victoria Park

7,5 /10

***a)** Imagine it is four o'clock on Wednesday. Look at the pictures and write down what the people have already done and what they haven't done yet.*

1

three boys – play football

2

people – listen to a concert

3

an old lady – read a book

4

mother and her two children – look at the deer

5

man – cut the grass

6

two tourists – visit the park

1 The three boys have ~~already~~ played football. 0,5
2 The people haven't listen to a concert yet.
3 An old lady has ~~already~~ read a book ~~ye~~ 0,5
4 A mother and her two children have ~~already~~ looked at the deer. 0,5
5 ~~A~~ the man hasn't cut the grass yet.
6 Two tourist have ~~Already~~ visited the park 0,5

***b)** Now write **four** questions to ask the two tourists and find out what they have done in the park today. Use **just, yet, ever**.*

3,5

1 Have you ever visited the Park before?
2 Have you seen the animals in the park yet?
3 Have you ever visited a Park?
4 Have you just climb at threes?

present perfect: questions

Have	you	**seen** the film yet?
What have	you	just **done**?
Why have	you	**come** to this cinema?

2 GRAMMAR About two tourists

8,5/11

You talk to two more tourists, Ricky and Kelly. Find out what they have done already and when they did it. Look at the pictures and complete the dialogues. Use the verbs in the box:

take a photo • go shopping • visit

1

Monday morning

You Have ✓ you already visited ✓ the London Eye?

Ricky and Kelly Yes, we have.

You When did you ~~do~~ visit it? −0,5

Ricky and Kelly We visited it on Monday.

2

Tuesday afternoon

You Have you already taken photos?

Ricky Yes, I have.

You When did you ~~do~~ take it? −0,5

Ricky I took ~~photos~~ it (✓) on Tuesday afternoon.

3

Tuesday afternoon

−1

You Have you already ~~gone~~ been shopping on a market?

Kelly yes, I have.

You When did you ~~do~~ it go shopping? −0,5

Kelly I went shopping on Tuesday afternoon.

present perfect und **simple past** im Vergleich

Wenn du sagen möchtest, dass du etwas schon gemacht hast, der Zeitpunkt ist dabei unwichtig: **present perfect**.
I have **already** visited the London Eye.

Wenn du den genauen Zeitpunkt nennst: **simple past**.
We visited it on **Monday morning**.

3 GRAMMAR A visit to the Tower

7 /7

It's 12 o'clock on a Saturday morning. There are lots of people at the Tower of London.
Look at the pictures and write down what people have been doing. Use ***since*** *or* ***for*** *in every sentence.*

1

stand there – 35 minutes

2

live at the Tower – a very long time

3

sell ice cream – this morning

4

walk up and down – 10 o'clock

5

look at the Crown Jewels – 20 minutes

6

watch boats on the river?

7

wait – 15 minutes

1 The people have been standing there for 35 minutes. ✓
2 The birds have been living at the Tower for a very long time. ✓
3 The woman has been selling ice cream since this morning ✓
4 The guard has been walking up and down since 10 o'clock. ✓
5 Man: "I 've been looking at the Crown Jewels for 20 min. ✓"
6 Mother: "How long have we been watching boats on the river?"
7 The guide has been waiting for 15 minutes. ✓

present perfect progressive

Verwendung
Wenn du sagen möchtest, dass etwas schon lange getan wird und noch immer andauert, verwendest du das **present perfect progressive**.

Bildung
has been oder **have been** + ing-Form **des verbs**
(He **has been** waiting. / They **have been** waiting.)

4 WORDS More information about Victoria Park

11,5 / 12

Read the sentences and fill in the missing words from the box. There are four more than you need. Be careful: sometimes you must also find the correct form of the word.

Messer

ending • strange • excited • plug • whistle • surprised • knife • open-air • victim • light • (to) be allowed to • (to) murder • button • flower • (to) appear • blood

erscheinen

Victoria Park is an old park in London. When you visit it for the first time, you'll be surprised at the many different trees and flowers there. Children are excited about the many different playgrounds[1] in the park. Last weekend an open-air theatre started. The play was a crime story[2] and many people came to watch it. It started when a young man came into a room and pulled out the plug so that there was no light. Then a second man appeared on the stage. He had a big knife in his right hand. Everybody thought that he wanted to murder the first man. But he just cut some bread and ate it. The victim was an old lady. She looked very strange. I'm not telling you the ending of the story! You must go and watch it yourself!

-0,5

Wörter richtig einsetzen!

Manche der Wörter oben im Kasten müssen verändert werden, d.h. dass
- bei einem Verb die richtige Zeit gebildet werden muss: z.B. play ▶ played
- bei einem Substantiv manchmal auch die Pluralform notwendig ist: z.B. button ▶ buttons

[1] playground ['pleɪgraʊnd] *Spielplatz* [2] crime story ['kraɪm ˌstɔːri] *Krimi*

MEDIATION

9 /10

Autumn in London

Dein Onkel und deine Tante planen anlässlich ihres Hochzeitstages am 24. Oktober einen Aufenthalt in London. Dein Onkel hat im Internet ein Angebot gefunden und bittet dich um deine Hilfe.

Come to London this autumn

A three-star hotel and organized sightseeing tours are waiting for you.
Choose your trip and enjoy some wonderful days in the capital of the United Kingdom.

You organize your flight to London … we do the rest. You will stay in our comfortable three-star hotel not far from the centre of London (Tube station near the hotel). Rooms include TV, telephone and private bathroom. Every day we will show you some wonderful sights in London. Is there a special reason why you are coming to London? Just tell us and we will have a surprise present waiting for you.

YOU CAN VISIT LONDON FOR THREE OR FOUR DAYS AND CHOOSE FROM THESE DATES: 2nd OCT, 14th OCT, 23rd OCT, 27th OCT		
DATE	THREE NIGHTS	FOUR NIGHTS
2nd OCT	*£155	£198
14th OCT	£150	£190
23rd OCT	£145	£185
27th OCT	£140	£180

* We serve you a special candlelit[1] dinner on the second evening of your visit.

Prices are for one person and include:

- three/four nights with breakfast and dinner in the hotel's restaurant and
- the following interesting sightseeing programmes:
  three nights: two half-day and one full-day sightseeing programme.
  four nights: two half-day and two full-day sightseeing programmes.
- If you are interested, we will organize the tickets for your evening activities (theatre, musical, cinema, …) and organize your transport. Or just spend the evening in our nice hotel bar.

Interested? Then what are you waiting for?
Do you want to find out more about our hotel and our sightseeing tours?

Fill in this form.

Name:

Address:

Telephone number:

E-mail

All the information will be in your mailbox in no more than three days.

[1] candlelit dinner ['kændllɪt] *romantisches Abendessen bei Kerzenschein*

Dein Onkel Ich habe hier ein Angebot in London gefunden. Es scheint sich um ein 3-Sterne-Hotel zu handeln. Aber viel mehr verstehe ich nicht. Ist ein Flug dabei und was steht da über die Hotelzimmer? (2P)

Du Den Flug musst du selber organisieren. Die Räume sind mit Fernseher, Telephon und einem privaten Bad.

Dein Onkel Wie sieht es mit der Verpflegung aus – welche anderen Mahlzeiten gibt es außer dem Frühstück? (1P)

Du Das Frühstück und das Abendessen

Dein Onkel Sie schreiben etwas über Aktivitäten am Abend. Gibt es auch ein organisiertes Abendprogramm? (3P)

Du Nein, aber sie können dir Karten/Tickets für Theather, Kinos oder Musicals besorgen

Dein Onkel Jetzt mal zu den Preisen. Ich sehe, dass es unterschiedliche Preise für drei oder vier Nächte gibt, das ist klar. Aber was bieten sie eigentlich zusätzlich an, wenn man vier Nächte bleibt? (1P)

Du Zwei halbtags und zwei ganztags Besichtigungsprogramme

Dein Onkel Und was bedeutet das Sternchen? (1P)

Du Wenn du ab 2. Oktober 3 Nächte buchst ist am 2. Abend ein romantisches Abendessen bei Kerzenschein dabei.

Dein Onkel Wo findet man etwas über das Besichtigungsprogramm? (2P)

Du Du musst das Formular ausfüllen, sie lassen dir die Informationen dann innerhalb 3 Tagen per E-mail zukommen.

SPEAKING

___/12

03 Talking to Dad

Josephine is a British girl. She is 14 years old and lives in a village not far from London.
Last week she went shopping in London with her friends.
When she comes home, her father wants to know everything.

Höre dir Josephines Antworten genau an und mache dir Notizen.
Sie helfen dir, wenn du in **Now you** Josephines Rolle übernimmst.

04 Now you

This time Josephine went to the Underage Festival in Victoria Park in London.
She is talking to her father. Again he wants to know everything. Take Josephine's part.

Before you start, think about the following things and make notes about ...

- who you went with
- how you got to London
- how you found your way to Victoria Park
- which line you took to Victoria Park (Tube station: Bethnal Green / ... line / ... bound)
- how much you paid for the entrance ticket for the *Underage Festival* (free)
- some details about the *Underage Festival* (bands, drinks, the kids' ages ...)
- when you got home – "no more questions"

Du kannst nochmals den Text „Victoria Park" auf S. 10 lesen. Dort findest du einige Informationen über das *Underage Festival*, die dir für diese Unterhaltung nützlich sein können.
Orientiere dich auch auf dem U-Bahn-Plan auf S. 14 in deinem Englischbuch.

Gesamtpunktzahl ______ /82	Note ______

READING

______ /17

Verschaffe dir zuerst einen Überblick, um was es in dem Text geht: Überschrift, Bilder, Text einmal lesen (**skimming**).
Lies dir dann die Aufgaben zum Text durch und suche nun anhand von Schlüsselwörtern gezielt nach den gefragten Informationen (**scanning**).

SCOTMAG – *your magazine for Scotland*

Going to school in Scotland

Dear readers,

In the coming weeks we want to tell you more about how students get to school. This week we are having a look at our students from Scotland. Many of our Scottish students go to school by bus or bike, but there are others …

Take Alice, 13, from the Isle of Flotta. She goes to school by ferry and bus – quite exciting, isn't it? It takes her about one and a half hours every Monday morning. That's why Alice stays at the school hostel during the week until she goes home again on Friday afternoon. Alice: "I miss my family a lot."

Going to school is a lot easier and quicker for Leo, 16, from Aberdeen. Leo's father is a taxi driver. He takes Leo to school every morning before he starts working. Leo likes it because he needn't get up so early. Leo: "It only takes me seven minutes to get to school, but sometimes I would like to spend some time before school on the bus together with my classmates."

Joel, 13, from Glasgow likes sleeping long – and he can sleep long every morning, because he lives right next to the school. Joel: "If I had a long journey to school, I would ask my parents to move nearer to the school. I hate getting up early."

Janet, 14, lives just outside Edinburgh and goes to school by train. She likes trains, stations and the different people at the stations. It takes her about half an hour to get to her school. Janet: "I enjoy my journey to school – I can read magazines and I have time to learn my German and French vocabulary."

Find out about Robert's funny way of going to school in next week's "SCOTMAG". We are interested in getting more information from Scottish students and from students from other parts of Britain or even from students abroad. Just tell us how you get to school, how long it takes you, if you like it or if you don't, and why. Please contact us by e-mail.

1 About going to school

___ / 6

Look at the pictures. Read the text and tick (✔) the ***six*** *things or situations that the text is about.*

2 The shortest journey to school

___ / 4

Write down numbers 1, 2, 3 and 4 next to the names below:
1 for the shortest and 4 for the longest time to get to school.

Alice 4

Leo 2

Joel 1

Janet 3

3 More about the article

___ / 7

Read the text again and find out if these sentences are right, wrong or not in the text.

	Right	Wrong	Not in the text
1 Every morning Alice goes to school by ferry.		✓	
2 Leo misses his friends in the morning.		✓	
3 Leo's father picks him up after school.			✓
4 Joel is quite happy with his journey to school.	✓		
5 Janet likes going by train.	✓		
6 The four students like school a lot.			✓
7 The magazine is looking for information from students in other countries too.		✓	

LANGUAGE

___ / 37

1 WORDS John Bennet, Isle of Flotta

___ / 13

a) *Fill in the missing words. They are all new in this unit.*
Be careful: in the box there are two more words than you need. (9P)

~~imagine~~ • ~~able to~~ • ~~great-grandmother~~ • ~~upset~~ • ~~during~~
~~once~~ • ~~salmon~~ • ~~scenery~~ • post • journey • ~~farmer~~

John Bennet lives on the Isle of Flotta. Hoy is a beautiful island with a wonderful ___scenery___.

He is a ___farmer___ and works on a ___salmon___ farm.

___During___ the trips with his boat, he often misses his wife and his daughter.

___Once___ a month the family visits Alice's ___great-grandmother___

Glenna Bennet in Kirkwall on Mainland. They must take the ferry to Mainland. The ferry leaves early in

the morning. As you can ___imagine___, Glenna Bennet is always happy when her

family comes. Sometimes John and his family aren't ___able to___ visit Glenna –

then she is very ___upset___.

b) *Explain the following two words in a complete sentence (4P):*

great-grandmother: ___She's the mother of your grandmother.___

___

journey: ___

___

2 WORDS Find the words.

___ / 6

Find the words and fill them in.

1 I was _ _ _ _ ☐ _ _ _ _ at the number of sea cages around Hoy.

2 There is only one shop on Hoy. They haven't got a ☐ _ _ _ _ _ ☐ _ _ _ _ _ _ ☐ _ _ _.

3 If you can't talk to a person on your mobile, you can send a ☐ _ _ _ _ _ _ _ _ ☐ _ _.

4 Katrina is _ _ _ _ ☐ because her mum won't pick her up on Friday.

5 It's difficult to _ _ ☐ _ _ ☐ _ a world without telephones.

6 If you put the letters in the boxes from 1–5 in the right order, you get a word for an exercise that you

sometimes do in your English lesson: ☐ ☐ ☐ ☐ ☐ l ☐ ☐ ☐ o ☐

3 GRAMMAR What would happen if …

_____ / 6

Complete the sentences. The following ideas in the box will help you.

be very unhappy • forget to learn it at home • sleep longer on Mondays
father not have a taxi • miss the train to Edinburgh • ????

1 If Alice lived in Kirkwall, ~~sche~~ she would sleep longer on Mondays.

2 Leo would go by bus If his father ~~hadn't~~ not had a taxi.

3 If Joel's parents moved to another part of the town, He would be very unhappy.

4 Janet would learn her German vocabulary on the train If she forgot to learn it at h.

5 Janet would be late If she missed the train to Edinburgh.

6 If I lived on the Isle of Hoy, I'd have a lot of animals like horses.

☞ **if-Sätze Typ 2 – „Was wäre, wenn …"**
Mit if-Sätzen Typ 2 kannst du ausdrücken, was unter bestimmten Bedingungen sein könnte, aber doch eher unwahrscheinlich ist (oder sogar unmöglich).

if-Satz (Bedingung)	**Hauptsatz (Folge)**
If I **won** a million euros,	I **would/could buy** a nice house for my family.
simple past	*would/could + infinitive*

4 GRAMMAR What is Alice saying?

_____ / 5

Look at the situations. What do you think Alice is saying? Use the words in the box.

go for a walk • correct • give • open • turn off

→

1 I'll send you my one.

2 I'll help you.

3

4

5

☞ Wenn man spontane Entschlüsse fasst oder jemandem spontan seine Hilfe anbietet, verwendet man das **will-future**.

5 GRAMMAR A busy weekend

___ /7

Look at the Bennets' family planner and write down what Alice, her brother and her parents are doing next weekend.

	Alice	Angus	John Bennet	Moyra Bennet
Friday	practise the fiddle for the ceilidh	watch Ice Age on DVD with his friends	pick up Alice from the ferry feed the salmon	plan the ceilidh
Saturday	play the fiddle at the ceilidh with Dad		play the fiddle at the ceilidh with Alice feed the salmon	make a cake for the evening
Sunday			feed the salmon	

1 On Friday Alice is going to practise the fiddle for the ceilidh.

2 On Saturday Alice is going to play the fiddle at the ceilidh with Dad.

3 On Friday Angus is going to watch Ice Age on DVD with his friends.

4 On Friday John Bennet is going to pick up Alice from the ferry... and Moyra B. is g. to plan the c.

5 On Saturday J.B. is going to play the fiddle

6 and M.B. is going to make a cake for the evening.

7 On Sunday J.B. is going to feed the salmon.

☞ Wenn du über **feste Pläne** oder **Verabredungen** in der Zukunft sprichst, kannst du das **present progressive** verwenden: *I'm going to Ashley party at the weekend.*
Um deutlich zu machen, dass es sich um zukünftige Pläne handelt, musst du **Zeitangaben** verwenden, z.B. *on Friday, next week, at the weekend, tomorrow ...*

STUDY SKILLS

_____ / 8

USING A DICTIONARY More information about Joel

You have to translate a few German sentences into English, but you don't know all the words. Use a dictionary and find the correct English words for the underlined German words.

☞ Lies immer erst den gesamten Wörterbucheintrag, bevor du dich für eine bestimmte Übersetzung entscheidest. Oft werden weitere Informationen gegeben, die du brauchst, um die richtige Übersetzung zu finden.

1 Joel interessiert sich für den Weltraum. (1P)

Joel is interested in ____________________.

2 Er liest viele Bücher über dieses Thema und sucht Informationen im Internet. (4P)

He reads many books on this ____________________ and ____________________

____________________ ____________________.

3 Letzte Woche hielt er sogar einen Vortrag darüber. (3P)

Last week he ____________________ ____________________ ____________________ about it.

WRITING

_____ / 20

A report for the school magazine

Together with his school orchestra, Leo went on a school trip to the "Music for Youth Festival" in Birmingham. There he met Katrina. After his trip he wrote a report about it for his school magazine.
Write Leo's report. Use the following ideas:

- Write about making friends on a school trip.
- Say who you are and what instrument you play (for how long – who started to teach you – where do you play now).
- Say what you did at the festival and how you felt.
- Tell the readers about your new friend Katrina (instrument – who taught her – about her father – where she goes to school).
- Say how you are going to keep in touch with her.
- Tell your readers what they can do to meet new friends.

☞
- Finde eine passende Überschrift.
- Beginne Leos Artikel mit einem einleitenden Satz, in dem du schreibst, worum es in dem Artikel geht.
- Fange für jeden neuen Gedanken einen neuen Abschnitt an. Denke daran, wenn möglich, deine Abschnitte jeweils mit einem **topic sentence** zu beginnen.
- Beende Leos Artikel mit einem abschließenden Satz oder einer Aufforderung an die Leser/innen.

Gesamtpunktzahl ohne Speaking ______ / 59	Note ______
Gesamtpunktzahl mit Speaking ______ / 76	Note ______

LISTENING

______ / 17

05 A presentation about Pitlochry, Scotland

Today Rick, one of Katrina's classmates, gives a presentation about Pitlochry, a small country town in Scotland. Listen to his presentation.

New word
ladder ['lædə] *Leiter*

1 The presentation

______ / 5

Look at the pictures. Listen to the text and put the pictures into the right order. Be careful: there are two more pictures than you need.

A
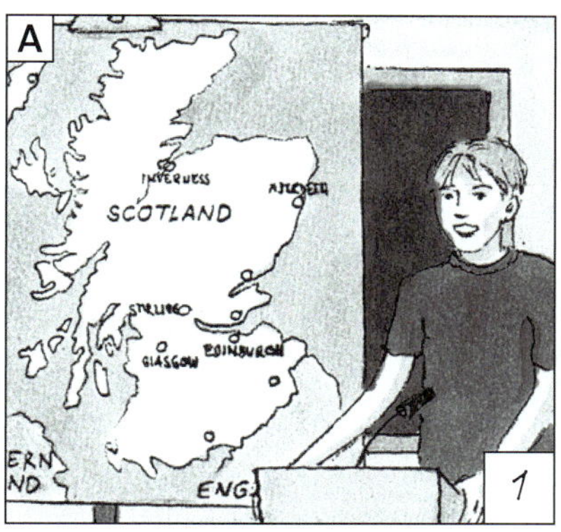

B

C

D

E

F
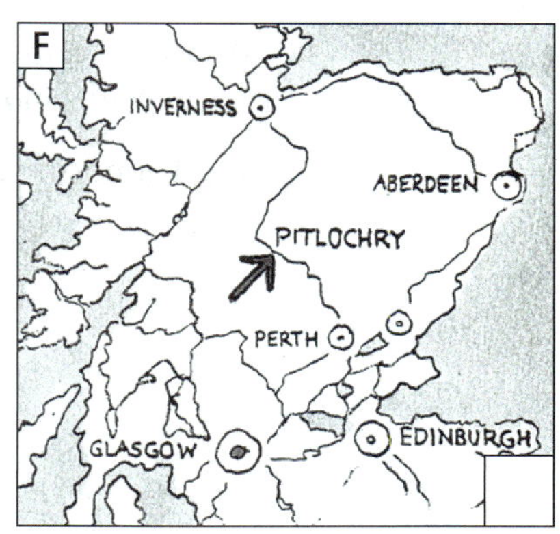

G

H

2 Come and spend your holidays in Pitlochry

___/8

Listen again. Match the sentence halves and draw lines.
Be careful: there are three more endings than you need.

1 Pitlochry is
2 Pitlochry looks
3 Many people come
4 You can explore the Highlands
5 Come and see
6 The Pitlochry Highland Games
7 If you come to Pitlochry,
8 People from all over the world

a) our famous salmon ladder!
b) if you are staying in Pitlochry.
c) to visit Pitlochry every year.
d) come to the Festival Theatre.
e) you will meet people from all over the world.
f) in the heart of Scotland.
g) a bit like 100 years ago.
h) to stay in caravans.
i) are an attraction for old and young people.
j) if you want to go snowboarding.
k) you will dance a lot.

3 Information about Pitlochry

___/4

Listen to the text again. Tick (✔) the right box.

1 At the beginning of his presentation Rick gives information about	the number of hotels in Pitlochry.	☐
	the structure of his presentation.	☐
	the youth hostel in Pitlochry.	☐

2 In Pitlochry	there are stone houses.	☐
	there are 2,800 people.	☐
	there are 3,500 people.	☐

3 Visitors to Pitlochry	can stay in a caravan.	☐
	never stay at hotels.	☐
	can stay at a Bed and Breakfast.	☐

4 If you visit the Pitlochry Highland Games,	you can watch Scottish sports.	☐
	you need an entrance ticket.	☐
	you will come in August.	☐

LANGUAGE

____ / 30

1 WORDS Just the opposite

____ / 5

Find the opposites:

1 remember ◄► forget

2 at the back ◄► at the front

3 above ◄► below

4 small ◄► big

5 begin ◄► end

2 WORDS Town and country

____ / 8

Label the pictures.

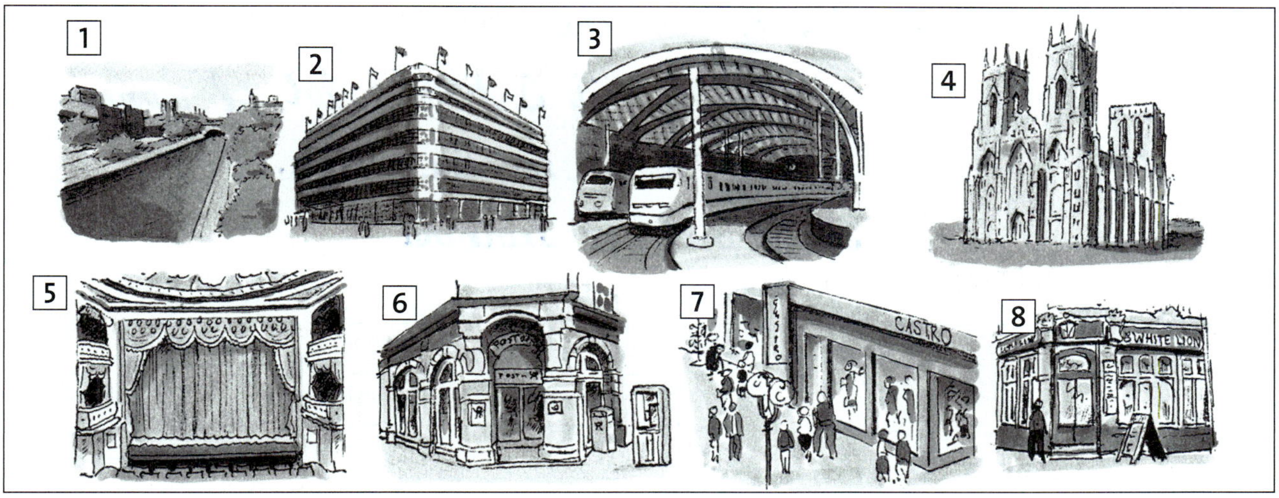

1 ____ 2 ____ 3 ____ 4 ____

5 theatre 6 ____ 7 ____ 8 ____

1 bay 2 cliff 3 church 4 lake

5 ____ 6 forest 7 waterfall 8 mountain

3 GRAMMAR Jason from Pitlochry

____ / 4

Jason thinks about what would happen if ... Complete his sentences.

1 If I lived in Australia, I ...
2 I would invite my family on a trip around the world if ...
3 If Manchester United played in Pitlochry, ...
4 I would take a photo of Nessie if ...

1 If I lived in Australia, I'd like to see the sea.
2 I would invite my family on a trip around the world if I have a lot of money.
3 If Manchester United played in Pitlochry, J'd go to the match..
4 I would take a photo of Nessie If I went to Scotland.

Hinweise zu **If-Sätzen Typ 2 – „Was wäre, wenn ..."** findest du in Klassenarbeit A auf S. 22.

4 GRAMMAR Jason needs help

____ / 6

Sometimes Jason needs help from other people. What do they say to him? Use the will-future.

1 ***Jason*** I forgot my pencils.
Ben I'll lend you my pencils (lend).

2 ***Jason*** I can't find my school bag.
Katrina I'll help you to look for it (help).

3 ***Jason*** I need a birthday present for my little brother.
Tom I'll go shopping with you (go shopping).

4 ***Jason*** I can't find my scissors[1].
Patricia I'll cut out the picture for you (cut out the picture).

5 ***Jason*** I've hurt my knee.
Mother I'll call the doctor (call the doctor).

Zum Gebrauch des **will-future** siehe Hinweis in Klassenarbeit A auf S. 23.

[1] scissors *(pl)* ['sɪzəz] *Schere*

5 GRAMMAR A holiday in Scotland

____/7

Jason's cousins from Manchester, Lee and Gregory, and their Dad want to go on a holiday to Scotland. Lee and Gregory have made some plans. They phone Jason to tell him what they are doing on which day. Use the following verbs and pictures.

visit • climb • listen to • walk • watch • eat • look for

1

Old Man of Hoy

2

path on the coast

3

pipers

4

Haggis

5

Nessie

6

Ben Nevis

7

Highland Games

1 On Monday morning we ____________________

2 On Tuesday afternoon we ____________________

3 On Wednesday we ____________________

4 On Thursday evening we ____________________

5 On Friday morning we ____________________

6 On Saturday we ____________________

7 On Sunday afternoon we ____________________

MEDIATION

____/12

Tickets for Pitlochry Festival Theatre

Buy Online

Steps to booking tickets online:

1. Click on the month you would like to come.
2. When you find the event you want, click 'Buy tickets'.
3. Next, choose the price and enter the number of tickets you want to buy.
4. Click 'Continue'.
5. Next you'll see a list of the tickets you have bought. Click 'Continue' if you are happy with your list or go back to 'Change' if not. Please note that you automatically get the best seats that are free – you cannot book special seats. This is something we hope to be able to offer in the future.
6. The next step is to enter your own personal details and the way you want to pay.
7. Click 'Buy tickets'.

DISCOVER ... TASTE ... HEAR ... TRY ... CREATE ... SEE ... DISCOVER ... TASTE ... HEAR ... TRY ... CREATE ... SEE ...

Your family is planning a trip to Scotland. You help your mother with the tickets for the Pitlochry Festival Theatre.

Deine Mutter Ich habe jetzt die Veranstaltung angeklickt, für die ich Karten kaufen will. Und was mache ich jetzt?

Du ____

____ (3P)

Deine Mutter Ah, jetzt sehe ich eine Liste mit den Karten. Aber Mensch, ich hab ja die falschen angeklickt! Kann ich das nochmal rückgängig machen?

Du ____

____ (2P)

Deine Mutter Gut, nochmal von vorne ... Ja, das sind jetzt die richtigen Karten. Jetzt möchte ich mir gerne noch Plätze aussuchen. Wie mache ich das?

Du ____

____ (3P)

Deine Mutter Und wie gehts jetzt weiter?

Du ____

____ (4P)

SPEAKING

____/17

06 Booking tickets on the phone

Mrs Baker is phoning the Pitlochry Festival Theatre booking office.
Listen to the dialogue.

Höre dir Mrs Bakers Antworten genau an und sprich sie nach. Mache dir Notizen. Sie helfen dir, wenn du im **Now you** selbst ein Telefongespräch führst.

07 Now you

You are staying with your penfriend Sue in Scotland. You want to go to one of the plays at Pitlochry Festival Theatre. Look at the programme and choose one of the plays. Then ring up the booking office and talk to the lady at the office.

	November		December		January		February		March
3	*Hot Chili Pepper*	1	*Sally and Joe*	6	*Sally and Joe*	2	*The Scottish Dream*	1	*A Bad Mistake*
12	*Ghosts*	2	*An Invitation*	10	*Ghosts*	8	*Hot Chili Pepper*	14	*An Invitation*
17	*Black and White*	15	*Hot Chili Pepper*	14	*Sally and Joe*	12	*An Invitation*	15	*Black and White*
25	*Hot Chili Pepper*	20	*Sally and Joe*	26	*The Scottish Dream*	20	*The Scottish Dream*	18	*An Invitation*
27	*Ghosts*	25	*Hot Chili Pepper*	27	*Ghosts*	22	*Hot Chili Pepper*	27	*A Bad Mistake*
30	*Black and White*	31	*An Invitation*	29	*The Scottish Dream*	27	*An Invitation*	30	*Black and White*

Falls du dir zum Buchstabieren deines Namens das englische Alphabet in Erinnerung rufen willst, findest du es in deinem Englischbuch auf S. 222.

Klassenarbeit A

Gesamtpunktzahl ohne Speaking ______ /75	Note ______
Gesamtpunktzahl mit Speaking ______ /95	Note ______

READING

______ /11

Die erste Aufgabe zum Lesetext auf S. 33 hilft dir, einen ersten Überblick zu bekommen, um was es in der Broschüre geht. Lies also zuerst Aufgabe 1 und überfliege dann den Text anhand der Überschriften, der Bilder und des ersten Satzes jedes Abschnitts.

Sports and English – teenage holiday camps

About us

We are a great team of young people who organize two-week summer camps in Germany.

We want young people from all over Germany to have fun with English, enjoy all kinds of sports and spend two weeks outdoors. This year camps will be in Freiburg, Rostock, Munich and Dresden.

English is fun

The language in the camps is English so you have the chance to speak English all day. From Monday to Friday there are also special English courses every morning (90 minutes). There are only six to ten students in one group.

Don't expect boring school lessons! No, we want you to have fun with English. We listen to the English radio news, watch English films, read the newspaper. We talk, discuss and … sing. All our teachers are native speakers[1] who help you to make the most of your abilities. All our teachers also speak German fluently.

Sport is fun

There are lots of activities that you can choose from. During the first two days of your stay we will show you all kinds of sports – football, tennis, baseball, table tennis, surfing*, swimming, hockey, volleyball and aerobics. On the third day you decide what you are going to concentrate on: you choose one main sport activity. You can add one or two activities that you would like to get to know better.

* Please note that surfing is only possible in the Rostock camp.

Daily life is fun

You will sleep in tents and we will cook our own meals together. We want to be good sportspeople so alcohol, cigarettes and drugs[2] are not allowed in the camp.

- **Last year more than 800 teenagers between 12 and 17 from all over Germany came to our camps.**
- **Come and join one of our camps this year!**
- **Find out more and visit our website: www.sports&english.com**

SPECIAL OFFER €490

[1] native speaker [ˌneɪtɪv ˈspiːkə] *Muttersprachler/in* [2] drugs [drʌgz] *Drogen*

1 What is the brochure about?

___/1

Tick (✔) the right statement.

The brochure is about ...

... teenagers in a British summer camp.	
... learning English in an outdoor summer camp.	
... summer camps where you do lots of sport activities and learn English.	✓
... how sporty students spend their summer holidays in England.	

2 Susanna is interested in the camp

___/10

Susanna from Freiburg has read the brochure. Now she is telling her English teacher at school all about it. Complete her sentences with information from the text.

1 The camps are in Freiburg, Rostock, Munich and Dresden.

2 The teenagers come from all over Germany.

3 They sleep in tents and they cook their own meals together.

4 In the camp you are not allowed to bring alcohol, cigarettes and drugs.

5 You learn English in small groups, there are only six to ten students.

6 In the English courses they learn English with good teachers, and for example they listen to the English radio news or read the newspaper. *(Write two facts.)*

7 The teachers speak German fluently.

8 After the second day you decide what you are going to concentrate on.

9 You can go surfing in Rostock camp.

Sätze vervollständigen (Completing sentences)
Bei dieser Aufgabenform musst du auf zwei Dinge achten: auf den Inhalt **und** auf die grammatikalische Korrektheit. Das bedeutet, dass du den vorgegebenen Satzanfang so ergänzen musst, dass sich ein vollständiger, richtiger Satz ergibt.

LANGUAGE

____/33

1 WORDS Camp activity: football

____/5

*Collect words that are linked with football and add them to this mind map. Find at least **ten** words.*

Du kannst in dieser Mindmap selbstständig weitere Äste ergänzen.

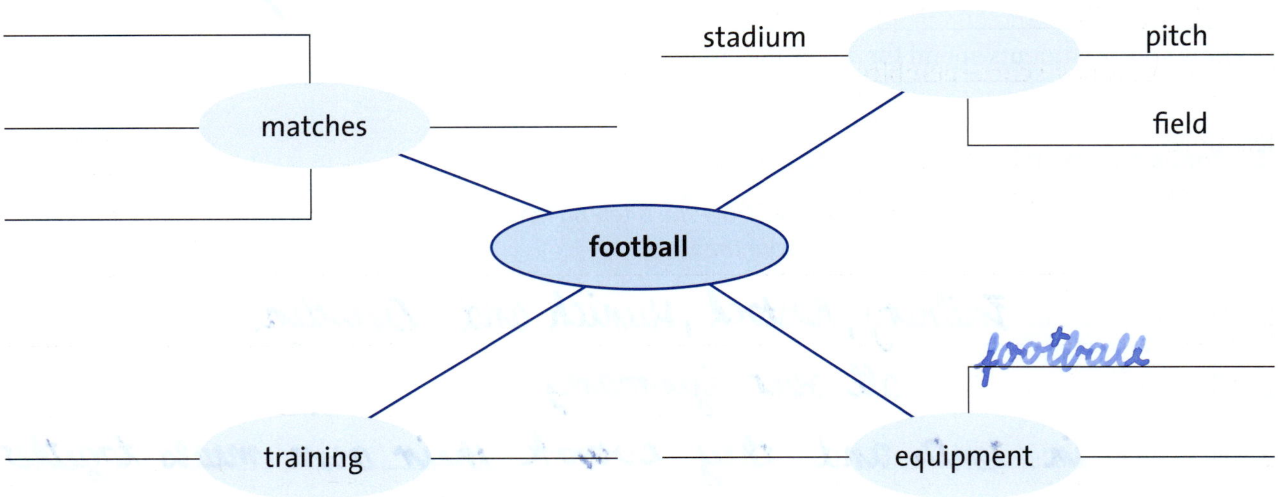

2 WORDS More sports

____/10

a) *What four sports can you see in the pictures?*
Write down the equipment that you need too and where you do each sport. (6P)

sport	equipment	location
tennis	tennis bat	sportshall
skaten	skateboard	skaterpark
table tennis	table-tennis bat	sportshall
swimming	swimsuit	swimming hall

b) *Choose **two** sports. Write two sentences about each sport. Write where you do it and what you need. (4P)*

Example:

You play table tennis in a sports hall. You need a table tennis bat.

1 You swim in a swimming pool. You need a swimsuit.

2 You skate in a skaterpark. You need a skateboard.

3 GRAMMAR Susanna and the camp

___/10

a) *Write sentences. Use* ***who*** *or* ***which****. (5P)*

1 Susanna / student / comes from Freiburg

2 Susanna / the only student / came to the camp by bus

3 Tennis and football / the two activities / Susanna chose on the third day

4 Aerobics / a sport / many girls in the camp chose as their favourite activity

5 Mike / English teacher / always starts the lesson with a song

6 Nate / only boy / chose aerobics

Example:

1 Susanna is a student who comes from Freiburg.

2 Susanna is the only student who came to the camp by bus.

3 Tennis and ~~to~~ football ~~are~~ were the two activities which Susanna chose on the third day.

4 Aerobics ~~is~~ was a sport which many girls in the camp chose as their favourite activity.

5 Mike was an English teacher who always starts the lesson with a song.

6 Nate was the only boy who chose aerobics.

b) *Finish these sentences and use* ***who*** *or* ***which****. (2P)*

1 Frank is a student who learns a lot for school.

2 Basketball is a sport which you have to run a lot.

„who" oder **„which"?**

who in Relativsätzen, die **Personen** beschreiben:
The **girl who** plays football well is called Nina.

which in Relativsätzen, die **Dinge** (und namenlose Tiere) beschreiben.
The **book that** I read was a present from my sister.

c) *Look at the following sentences and put the relative pronouns* ***which*** *or* ***who*** *in brackets ( ) if you can leave them out. (3P)*

1 All the activities (which) you can choose are great fun.

2 English is the language which is spoken in all the camps.

3 All 800 teenagers who came to the camps last year were from Germany.

4 Surfing is the sport (which) you can only do in Rostock.

5 The people (who) you meet at the camp are all between 12 and 17.

6 Teenagers who want to be good sportspeople don't drink alcohol.

4 GRAMMAR The camp on the internet

___ /8

a) *Susanna has found a report from a German student who went to the camp in Rostock last year. This is the information she finds most interesting. Put in the* ***simple past passive form*** *of the verb.*

1 A new camp was opened (open) in Rostock last year.

2 Some teenagers were taken (take) to the seaside to go surfing.

3 Tennis was chose (choose) a lot because the camp had new tennis courts.

4 Many English films were showed (show) in the evenings.

b) *Match the sentence halves and use a* ***simple past passive form*** *of the following verbs:*

teach • sell • start • play

1 Most lessons	at the camp kiosk.
2 A funny game	with an English song.
3 Cheap lemonade	in small groups.
4 All students	at the party on the last evening.

1 The most lessons were started with an English song.

2 A funny game was played at the party on the last evening

3 Cheap lemonade was sell at the camp kiosk.

4 All students were ~~teach~~ taughed in small groups.

Bildung des Passivs im simple past

were/was + past participle (die dritte Form des Verbs)

The meals were cooked in a large tent.
Basketball was offered in all the camps.

STUDY SKILLS

____/15

PARAPHRASING Susanna is getting by in English

a) *When Susanna speaks English, she sometimes doesn't know the correct English words. So she paraphrases them. (12P)*

Wenn du ein Wort umschreiben möchtest, kannst du so anfangen:
- It's something that ...
- It's a place where ...
- It's somebody who ...

1 Trainer

It's somebody who trains people for an important match.

2 Friseur

It's somebody who cuts hair. ~~and~~

3 Gemeindehalle

It's a place where all people can go there, often in the central city.

4 Durchsage

It's something that ~~a lot of~~ a person makes, if a lot of people have to do sth...

5 Helm

It's something that you wear if you ride your bike or a horse.

6 Bahnsteig

It's a place where you get on and off a train.

b) *Now tell Susanna the correct English words. (3P)*

1 coach

2 hairdresser

3 community hall

4 announcement

5 helmet

6 platform

MEDIATION

____/16

Summer camp scholarship[1] – information for parents

Dear parents,
Once again there are scholarships that families with three or more children can ask for. There is a total amount[2] of €5,000 that we will give those families who have asked for scholarships. So it is important that you apply[3] for the scholarship early in the year. Please understand that you can only apply for one scholarship even if more than one of your children wants to join our camps.

What you should do

★ You may apply for not more than €200.

★ Tell us the amount of money you are asking for.

★ Apply before 1 May.

★ Tell us your name, address, the number of children in your family, the name and date of the camp.

★ Tell us the amount of money your family can spend every month.

★ Your son or daughter should write a short essay on why he or she wants to join one of our camps.

★ Send everything to our office in Hamburg.

★ Wait for our answer.

What you should know

★ After you have applied for the scholarship please don't call our organization. Please wait for more information. Although we try to answer letters quickly, sometimes it takes three or four weeks.

★ If your family got a scholarship last year, the earliest date for another scholarship is next year. Sorry!

★ You can be sure that nobody in the camp will know that your family got a scholarship.

Your kids will spend two unforgettable weeks in one of our camps – so what are you waiting for?

Yours sincerely,

Pete Wyatt
Director of Scholarship for Camps

[1] scholarship *Stipendium (= finanzielle Unterstützung für Schüler/innen)* [2] amount *Betrag* [3] to apply for *sich bewerben um*

You want to go to a summer camp. Today you are talking to your parents and explain how you can apply for a scholarship.

Papa Wer kann sich überhaupt um eine solche Unterstützung bewerben?

Du ______________________________ (1P)

Mama Wie viel Geld steht insgesamt zur Verfügung und wie viel könnten wir als Familie bekommen?

Du ______________________________ (2P)

Papa Welche Angaben muss man bei der Bewerbung machen?

Du ______________________________

____

______________________________ (4P)

Mama Muss man der Bewerbung sonst noch etwas beilegen?

Du ______________________________ (2P)

Papa Wann müssen wir uns bewerben?

Du ______________________________ (1P)

Mama Und wie geht es dann weiter?

Du ______________________________ (2P)

Papa Kann man da jedes Jahr einen neuen Antrag stellen?

Du ______________________________ (2P)

Papa Gibt es sonst noch etwas Wichtiges, was wir wissen sollten?

Du ______________________________ (2P)

SPEAKING

____/ 20

08 Getting to know the other teenagers at the camp

In the afternoon of the first day all the teenagers at the camp in Rostock meet.
First they talk in pairs, take notes and then everybody introduces[1] another teenager to the group.
Listen to Matthias, who introduces Valentin.

Höre dir Matthias' Vorstellung an und sprich sie abschnittsweise nach.
Notiere dir hilfreiche Formulierungen für deine eigene Vorstellung im **Now you**.

Now you

Imagine you are at a camp too. Now you introduce another teenager. Invent[2] a name and other personal details.
Use this notepad and make some notes before you speak.

Name ____________________

Age ____________________

Where from ____________________

- ***town/city/village*** ____________________
- ***where in Germany*** ____________________

Brothers or sisters ____________________

School ____________________

- ***languages*** ____________________
- ***favourite subject*** ____________________
- ***...*** ____________________

What he/she wants to be
(Schlage in einem Wörterbuch einen Beruf nach.) ____________________

____

Why here at the camp ____________________

Favourite sport ____________________

Sport he/she wants to do at the camp + why ____________________

____

[1] (to) introduce sb. [ˌɪntrəˈdjuːs] *jn. vorstellen* [2] (to) invent sth. [ɪnˈvent] *etwas erfinden*

Gesamtpunktzahl ______ / 60 Note ______

LISTENING

______ / 11

9 A visit to the Lowry

There is an advert[1] on the radio about the Lowry. Listen to it.

New words
painting ['peɪntɪŋ] *Gemälde*
puzzle ['pʌzl] *Rätsel*

Die erste Aufgabe zum Hörverstehenstext hilft dir, einen ersten Überblick zu bekommen, um was es in dem Werbespot geht. Lies die Aufgabe also vor dem ersten Hören, damit du sie dann leicht lösen kannst.

1 About the advert

______ / 1

Listen to the advert and then tick (✔) the right statement.

The advert is about ...

... the address of the Lowry.	
... the painter Lowry.	
... going to the Lowry with the whole family.	✔
... the times when you can visit the Lowry.	

[1] advert ['ædvɜːt] *Werbespot*

2 About the Lowry

___/5

Tick (✔) the right statement.

The Lowry is	only open for families.	
	a good place for families.	✔
	only for small children.	

The rucksacks	are a great help for families.	✔
	are not allowed in the museum.	
	are good for food and drinks.	

Next month there will be	a drama workshop.	✔
	activities for telling stories.	
	postcards with Lowry's paintings.	

In December	there are no workshops.	
	families don't pay to visit the museum.	
	Sundays are free for families.	✔

In the Lowry	you can go to the restaurant.	✔
	you can buy postcards.	
	you must have a rucksack.	

3 At home

___/5

Listen to the advert again. Sabrina has visited the Lowry.
Now she is at home again and her friend asks her questions about the Lowry.
Answer the questions. You can write short answers – you needn't write complete sentences.

1 Families can get rucksacks in the Lowry. What is in the rucksacks? *(Write two things.)*

____

2 There are two different workshops in the Lowry this month. What can you do there? *(Write two facts.)*

____

3 What is special about the "Free Family Sunday"?

____

STUDY SKILLS

____ / 6

PARAPHRASING Talking about the Lowry

An expert from the Lowry talks about the museum. Choose three of the words and explain them.

painter • "Free Family Sunday" • the Lowry • creative workshops • story-telling workshop

So kannst du deine Erklärungen beginnen:
- … is something
- … is a person/somebody
- … is a place/room
- … is a day

Wenn du für deine Worterklärung Informationen benötigst, findest du sie im Hörtext auf S. 27 in den Lösungen.

1 ______________________________ (2P)

2 ______________________________ (2P)

3 ______________________________ (2P)

LANGUAGE

____ / 23

1 GRAMMAR More information about the Lowry

____ / 9

***a)** Use the verb and the information from the boxes to write a relative clause. (6P)*

Example:
Children like the story-telling workshop best. be under ten years old
Children who are under ten years old like the story-telling workshop best.

1 The "Family Corner" is a great place. like many families

____

2 Mr L. S. Lowry was born in Manchester. be a painter

____

3 Every month there are new workshops. can join you

____

4 The Lowry souvenirs are very nice. be sold at the gift shop

____

5 The Lowry offers info-rucksacks. must get from the information desk visitors

____

6 The website gives you the opening hours. show a lot information on the Lowry

____

→

b) Read your sentences again. Write down the numbers of the sentences where you can leave out ***who*** *or* ***which****. (3P)*

| 1 | 3 | 5 |

2 GRAMMAR Last month at the Lowry

____ / 6

Look at the calendar from the secretary's office at the Lowry.
Make ***passive sentences*** *about what happened* ***last month****.*

Fri	12	order some new chairs (Mrs Baker)
Sat	13	
Sun	14	welcome group of art students from Edinburgh (Mr Smith and Mrs Kelly)
Mon	15	clean windows (the CleanWindow Company)
Tue	16	
Wed	17	plan project: "art for youth" (director of arts)
Thu	18	design website (creative team)
Fri	19	paint cafeteria (caretaker)

1 On Friday 12 some new chairs ~~was~~ are ordered by Mrs Baker.

2 On Sunday 14 a group of art students was welcomed by Mr S. and Mrs K.

3 On Monday 15 the windows were cleaned by the CleanWindow Company.

4 On Wednesday 17 the project "art for youth" was planned by the director of arts.

5 On Thursday 18 the website was designed by the creative team.

6 On Friday 19 the cafetaria was painted by the caretaker.

Wenn du in einem Passivsatz den „Täter" oder „Verursacher" nennen willst, verwendest du die Präposition **by** („von", „durch")

3 WORDS Find the words

___ /8

1
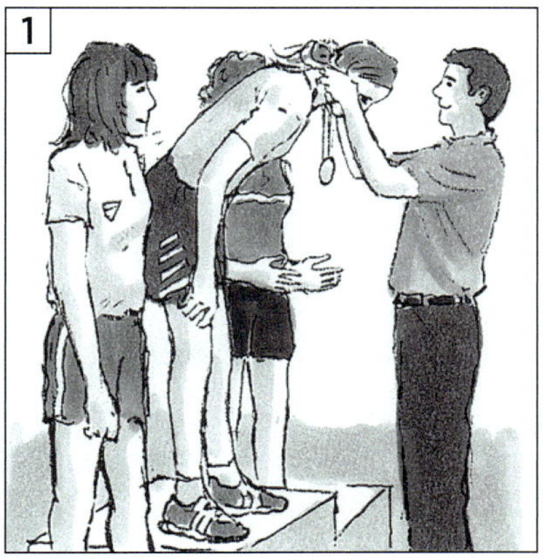

2

3

4

5

6

7

Find the words and fill them in.

1 The winner got the gold m e d a l.
2 Can you help me to u n l o a d the car? It's full of bags.
3 I've had these flowers since last year – they are a r t i f i c i a l.
4 Peggy had an accident with her bike – we had to call the a m b u l a n c e.
5 She had an o p e r a t i o n on her knee.
6 Larry is a good g o a l k e e p e r.
7 This summer our team won the c h a m p i o n s h i p.

Can you make a word out of the letters in the boxes from 1–7? Sentence 8 will help you.

8 I love sports like running and jumping – I love a t h l e t i c s.

WRITING

___/20

A day out to the Lowry

Imagine you are a student at a school in Leeds. Yesterday you went on a day out to the Lowry in Manchester. You write a report about your visit to the Lowry for the school magazine.

☞
- Denke dir eine interessante Überschrift aus.
- Schreibe am Anfang, um was es in deinem Bericht geht. Die Details kommen später.
- Mache an geeigneten Stellen einen Abschnitt.
- Beende deinen Bericht mit einem abschließenden Satz.
- Denke daran, das **simple past** zu verwenden.

In your report answer these questions:

– Who?	students of Form 7 LM
– What event was it?	a day out
– Where?	to the Lowry in Manchester – building amazing
– When?	February 25th, from 10 am to 2 pm – by train – nice walk to the museum – sunshine
– Why?	do a presentation about the famous painter L. S. Lowry, find out about him, collect information, copy one of Lowry's paintings
– How?	very interesting, different games and activities around the paintings, some students: design their own postcards
– What happened?	a boy – touch painting – alarm – police – not arrest

Art is cool

In February 25th our class, the students of Form 7 LM visited the Lowry in Manchester.

Gesamtpunktzahl ______ / 74 Note ______

READING

______ / 13

http://www.avh.montreal.qc.ca

avh

Alexander von Humboldt (AvH) German International School Montreal

Alexander von Humboldt German International School is a private school in Montreal, Canada. We have a large science and arts program[1] for all children from kindergarten to high school[2]. Many of our students have German parents or grandparents and so speak some German at home. However, not all our students have a German background – of course our school welcomes students of all nationalities. We also welcome guest students from Europe in year 10.

Children who don't speak German are welcome at our kindergarten. There they can learn the German language easily from other German-speaking children and of course from our language program. The kindergarten is open three days a week for children from the age of 2½ to 3½, and on five days a week for children from 3½ to 5.

Languages are very important at Alexander von Humboldt School. So our teachers at AvH do not only teach three languages, they teach **in** three languages: German, French and English. This helps every student to speak the three languages very well. While German plays an important role in the first years, English and French become more important in the higher years. After year 11 students can take the Canadian High School Diploma. In year 12 students will have the chance to take the German International Abitur.

The school was opened in 1980. Today 310 students from many different countries are learning in a friendly atmosphere. Lessons can be in the classroom, but very often outside the classroom too. The little ones have sleepovers in the school, for example a book night. There are 3 full-day field trips in the country, ski trips and visits to museums, music and theatre concerts for the older students. Of course, students go abroad during their time at Alexander von Humboldt International School. There is a study trip to Germany for up to 11 days in year 8. In year 9, students can go on a study trip to New York City for four days.

Parents are an important part of our school – we want parents to play an active role and help their children make the best out of their time at Alexander von Humboldt.

Interested? Then come to our

OPEN HOUSE

October 17 and January 16

9 am – 4 pm.

We have two Open Houses a year, in October and January. Have a walk round our school and see the building with its classrooms, science and art rooms and the library. Watch our students working with our modern computers. Visit the cafeteria and you'll meet teachers, students and parents.

Come and get to know our excellent school. We will be happy to meet you at AvH.

[1] program = *amerikanische Schreibweise für* programme [2] high school ['haɪ sku:l] *(USA, Kanada) Schule für 14–18-Jährige*

1 What is the website about?

___ / 1

What is this website about? Read it and tick (✔) the correct statement. Only one answer is correct.

This website tells you about …

… how you can find online friends at a Canadian school.	
… how German and Canadian schools work together.	
… what the school offers[1] to students.	✓
… how parents and students prepare the Open House.	

2 About AvH

___ / 6

Match these headings to the paragraphs 1–6. Find the best headings.
Be careful: there are three headings that you don't need.

A Activities for the students
B AvH's history
C Calendar and events
D Find out more about our school
E International contacts
F Learn different languages
G Parents support their children
H Start with German
I The students' nationalities[2]

1	2	3	4	5	6
I	F	H	B	G	D

3 More details about AvH

___ / 6

Anwer the questions on the text. You can write short answers – you needn't write complete sentences.

1 Where do the children at AvH come from?

From Germany, but however, not all of them.

2 Where can the children learn German?

In kindergardens or schools with german children.

3 What languages can the students at AvH learn?

German, French and English

4 What do the little ones do when they sleep in the school?

sleepovers, for example a book-night

5 What is special about Years 8 and 9?

study trips

6 What can visitors to the Open House see? (Write three facts.)

classrooms, science and art rooms, library

[1] (to) offer ['ɒfə] *anbieten* [2] nationality [ˌnæʃə'næləti] *Nationalität*

LANGUAGE

____ / 41

1 WORDS A school discussion

____ / 9

Last week there was a discussion at AvH about teenagers and their parents.
Here are some of the statements.
Complete them with the words from the box.
There are three words in the box that you don't need.
Be careful: you must find the correct form if a word is underlined.

agree • argument • blame for • cellphone • crazy • disagree • late • per • hang out • strict • traditional • waste

1 Twenty years ago family life in Canada was very __waste__.

2 Parents were __strict__ and children had to help a lot in the house.

3 Teenagers always want the __traditional__ clothes.

4 My children talk to their friends on their ________ a lot.

5 In her last holidays my daughter ________ a lot of time in front of the computer.

6 You can't ________ the children ________ modern technology.

7 My 14-year-old son always __hang out__ with his friends in the park.

8 One hour __per__ day in front of the computer is enough.

9 Some teenagers are __crazier__ about computer games than other kids are.

☞ Bei dieser Übung musst du bei manchen Wörtern auch die richtige Form finden.
Sieh dir die folgende Liste an, um dir die möglichen Veränderungen klarzumachen:

Verben	Form Zeit	meet ▶ he meets (he, she, it ▶ das S muss mit) meet ▶ they met (simple past), ...
Nomen	Singular oder Plural	child ▶ children
Adjektive	Steigerung	careful ▶ more careful; silly ▶ sillier

2 GRAMMAR Facts about AvH

____/8

Complete the following information about AvH. (Look at the text on AvH again if necessary.)
Use a verb from the box for each statement. Use the passive in the ***simple present*** *or the* ***simple past****.*

invite • teach (2x) • name • organize • accept[1] • show • open

1 At AvH subjects ~~were~~ are taught ____ in three different languages.

2 Students from all nationalities ~~were~~ are accept ____ at AvH.

3 AvH was opened ____ in 1980.

4 Last year many different field trips were organized ____ for older students.

5 Parents ~~were~~ are invited ____ to take an active role at AvH.

6 At Open House the whole school is showed ____ to interested visitors.

7 AvH ~~was~~ is named ____ after the German scientist Alexander von Humboldt.

8 German ~~was~~ is taught ____ at kindergarten to children without a German background.

Das Passiv (The Passive)
In **Passivsätzen** drückst du aus, dass etwas mit einer Person oder einer Sache geschieht.

Das **Passiv** bildest du mit einer Form von *be* und der 3. Form des Verbs (past participle):
simple present: am/are/is + past participle:
The school is named ... / The students are taught ...
simple past: was/were + past participle:
The school was built ... / The computers were bought ...

[1] (to) accept [ək'sept] *annehmen*

3 GRAMMAR Open House at AvH School

____ / 16

Janet has written an article about the Open House at her school for the school magazine. Put in the correct forms of the ***simple past*** *or the* ***past perfect****.*

The Open House on 16 March was (be) a really exciting day at AvH. After we had met (meet) in the classroom at 8 am, our form teacher Mrs Martin gave out (give out) some worksheets. She wanted (want) to show the visitors how we prepare for tests. Long before the visitors arrived (arrive) we had started (start) with our work and everything had been (be) quiet, but then some visitors came (come) in. First we felt (feel) a bit strange with all those people in the room. But it was (be) OK later. Form 8 HD presented (present) their project "First steps in the kitchen" which they had prepared (prepare) the week before. At the beginning of the week they learned (learn) how to cook some easy meals. After they had done (do) that they mad (make) posters about cooking. Because a boy from 8 FC had seen (see) a bear during his camping holiday last summer his form produced (produce) a booklet about how campers can go camping safely.

past perfect

Mit dem **past perfect** drückst du wie mit dem Plusquamperfekt im Deutschen aus, dass eine Handlung noch vor einer anderen Handlung in der Vergangenheit stattgefunden hat. Die Handlung im **past perfect** geschah zuerst.

Man bildet das **past perfect** mit *had* und der 3. Form des Verbs (Past Participle):

2 … 1

Robert went to the mall, because he had decided to buy a present for his mum.

1 … 2

He had already chosen a present when Sam came in.

4 GRAMMAR Interviews at Open House

___/8

Janet also interviewed some people at Open House at AvH. This is what they said:

1 I really liked the presentations about so many different topics.

2 I don't speak much German. But I want to work hard to learn it.

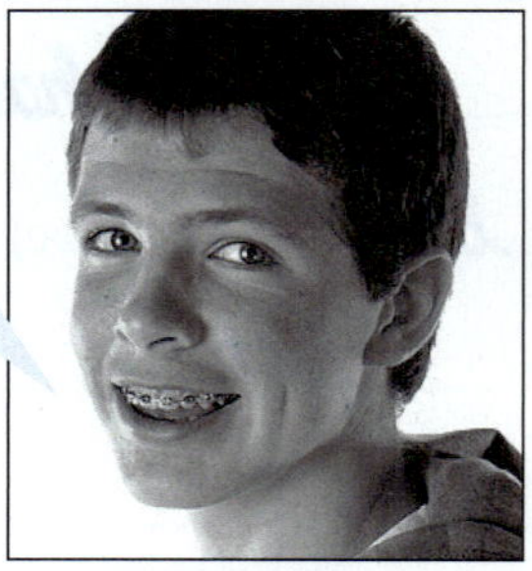

3 My sister and I came here much earlier than on a normal school day because we had to prepare our presentation.

4 We are going to send our son to this school next year. Hopefully, he will be happy here.

5 We haven't been able to show all our exciting experiments.

The next day Janet reports to her class what people in the interview told her. Write indirect sentences for Janet's report. Use different reporting verbs: say, tell, explain.

Indirect Speech (Indirekte Rede)
Die **einleitenden Verben** stehen hier alle im **simple past**. Denke also an die daraus resultierenden Zeitverschiebungen (backshift of tenses). Im Grammar File 11 auf Seite 160 in deinem Englischbuch findest du eine Übersicht über die Zeitverschiebungen. Denke außerdem an die sich verändernden Personalpronomen.

1 A mother said that she really liked the presentations about so many d. topics (1P)

2 A boy said that ______ (1P)

He explained that ______ (1P)

3 A girl ______

______ (2P)

4 A father ______

______ (2P)

5 A teacher ______ (1P)

WRITING

____/20

An e-mail about a school trip

Your German school has got a partner school in Canada. You often write e-mails to each other about what happens at your school. Today you want to tell the Canadian students about your last school trip.

Write about

– where you went, your journey, where you stayed

– what it was like, the people, what you were allowed / not allowed to do, the food, your teachers

Use the simple past.

You can start like this:

Dear friends,
Guess what we did last month! We ...

Steps of Writing

Rufe dir die Schritte beim Verfassen eines Textes in Erinnerung:

1. Vor dem Schreiben: Brainstorming
   - Sammle zunächst alle Ideen, die dir einfallen, z. B. in einer Mindmap oder einer Liste.
   - Wähle dann die besten Ideen aus und ordne sie.
2. Während des Schreibens:
   - Gestalte die Einleitung so, dass sie für die Leser interessant ist und zum Weiterlesen einlädt.
   - Gliedere deinen Text in Einleitung, Mittelteil und Schluss.
   - Denke daran, einen Absatz zu machen, wenn du mit einer neuen Idee anfängst. Und beginne jeden Absatz mit einem einleitenden Satz *(topic sentence)*.
   - Benutze treffende Adjektive: *strict, excellent, ...* und Adverbien: *nervously, quickly, ...*
   - Benutze Konjunktionen: *although, and, because, but, so ... that, when, while.*
   - Benutze time phrases: *at 7 o'clock, every morning, in the afternoon(s), a few minutes later, suddenly, then, next.*
   - Benutze Relativsätze mit *who, which* und *that.*
   - Benutze Sätze im Passiv.
3. Nach dem Schreiben:
   - Überprüfe, ob dein Text verständlich ist.
   - Überprüfe die Rechtschreibung.
   - Überprüfe die Verbformen (z. B. simple past) und die Wortstellung.

Klassenarbeit B

Gesamtpunktzahl ohne Speaking ______ / 69 Note ______

Gesamtpunktzahl mit Speaking ______ / 89 Note ______

LISTENING

____ / 21

10/11 New contest at Radio CBC 1, Montreal

New word
(to) protect [prə'tekt] *schützen*

10 1 Kids' Club on Radio CBC 1

____ / 5

Listen to Radio CBC 1. You are going to hear a report about a contest for children.

a) *At Victoria School, Toronto, three different classes are working on different projects. Tick (✔) which class is working on the Radio CBC 1 contest.*

One class is writing a diary about their two-week camp near Ontario.	☐
One class is making posters about how people can use public transport[1] more often and in this way help to keep the air of our country clean.	☐
One class is working on a musical about the life of young people in Canada.	☐

b) *Listen again. Tick (✔) the right box.*

1 Radio CBC 1 has a contest	a) every month.	☐
	b) twice a year.	☐
	c) every year.	☐
	d) every 2nd year.	☐
2 The contest is for kids	a) from 6 to 12.	☐
	b) from 6 to 16.	☐
	c) from 10 to 16.	☐
	d) in form 6.	☐
3 You can hand in	a) films.	☐
	b) computer shows.	☐
	c) stories and poems.	☐
	d) interviews.	☐
4 You will get more information about the contest	a) on their website.	☐
	b) in the next show.	☐
	c) from the radio's magazine.	☐
	d) if you write an e-mail.	☐

[1] public transport [ˌpʌblɪk 'trænspɔːt] *öffentliche Verkehrsmittel*

11 2 At Victoria School, Toronto

____ / 16

Mrs Riley, form teacher of year 7 at Victoria School, Toronto, is talking about the contest to her students.

a) *What is Mrs Riley talking about to her class? Tick (✔)* ***Yes*** *or* ***No****. (6P)*

Mrs Riley is talking about ...	Yes	No
the rules[1] for writing.		
when they can use the computer room.		
when they can talk to their Art teacher.		
the rules for painting and drawing.		
what students have to do in class and at home.		
the prizes.		

b) *Listen again. Answer these questions. Write short answers. You don't have to write complete sentences.*

☞ Lies die Fragen vor dem Hören und markiere dir in jeder Frage Schlüsselwörter, die dir helfen, die gewünschte Information aus dem Hörtext herauszufiltern.

1 What is important when you want to write something? (Write two things.) (4P)

____

2 What are you not allowed to do? (3P)

____

3 By when do you need to hand in your work at school? (1P)

____

4 What are the prizes for the national winners? (2P)

____

LANGUAGE

____ / 34

1 WORDS opposites

____ / 5

Write the opposites of these words:

1 oldest ◂▸ ____________

2 to get sth. wrong ◂▸ ____________

3 agree ◂▸ ____________

4 child ◂▸ ____________

5 to shake your head ◂▸ ____________

[1] rule [ruːl] *Regel, Vorschrift*

2 GRAMMAR About the contest

____/6

*Make one sentence out of two, as this is better style. But be careful: you must decide which action came first. Use the **past perfect** to say what had happened first. The action which followed is in the **simple past**. Use the conjunctions given in brackets.*

1 Radio CBC 1, Montreal decided to have a new contest. A class from Victoria School took part. *(when)*

____

____

2 The class decided to take part in the contest. They found more information on CBC 1's website. *(before)*

____

____

3 Mrs Riley told the students what they had to do. The students started to work on their project. *(after)*

____

____

4 Mrs Riley told the class about the prizes. Sarah asked about them. *(because)*

____

____

5 The groups found titles for their projects. They wrote the titles down on white paper. *(after)*

____

____

6 The students thought about climate change[1]. They made posters about saving energy for every classroom. *(because)*

____

____

3 WORDS Paraphrased words

____/11

a) *Someone has paraphrased these words. Can you find them? (5P)*

1 It's somebody who has done something really special: ______________

2 It tells you how fast you are allowed to drive: ______________

3 It's a big place where you can buy things: ______________

4 It's something you might go through when you're canoeing: ______________

5 It's a person who looks after a national park: ______________

[1] climate change ['klaɪmət tʃeɪndʒ] *Klimawandel*

b) *Paraphrase these three words: (6P)*

☞ Beim Paraphasieren (Umschreiben) von Wörtern kannst du so beginnen:
It's something that ... / It's somebody who ... / It's a place where ...

volunteer work: ______________________________

stadium: ______________________________

adult: ______________________________

4 GRAMMAR An interview about the CBC 1 contest

___ / 12

A journalist from the Toronto Star spoke to some people at Victoria School about the CBC 1 contest. This is what he recorded.

1 ***Head teacher*** The contest is a great idea. It makes students think about the environment. (1P)

2 ***Girl*** I took part in the contest last year and won a prize. I'm going to take part again this year. (3P)

3 ***English teacher*** I will give students time in lessons to write their texts. (1P)

4 ***Inuit boy*** My people have always been close to nature. (1P)

5 ***Art teacher*** I'm helping my students to find the right material for their ideas. (1P)

6 ***Teacher*** I'm proud that so many students are interested in the contest. (2P)

7 ***Mother*** It's important that there is more than lessons at Victoria School. (2P)

8 ***Three boys*** Maybe our idea can really help Canada to become cleaner. (1P)

Now write his report. Use different reporting verbs: explain, promise, say, tell sb.

1 The head teacher said that the contest was a great idea ...

____

2 A girl told me ______________________________

3 ______________________________

4 ______________________________

5 ______________________________

6 ______________________________

7 ______________________________

8 ______________________________

MEDIATION

____/14

A contest in Germany

Sport an eurer Schule

Das Thema unseres diesjährigen Wettbewerbs ist „Sport an eurer Schule“.
Teilnehmen können alle Schülerinnen und Schüler im Alter von 10 bis 16 Jahren.

Ihr könnt

- ★ über den Sportunterricht an eurer Schule berichten (wann findet er statt, wie oft, was macht ihr im Sportunterricht, was habt ihr für Verbesserungsvorschläge?).
- ★ eine Geschichte über ein lustiges Ereignis während des Sportunterrichts schreiben.
- ★ einen Bericht über ein wichtiges sportliches Ereignis an eurer Schule schreiben.
- ★ ein Interview mit einem Schüler / einer Schülerin machen, der/die eine Lieblingssportart hat. Erstellt eine Tondatei des Interviews oder schreibt es auf.
- ★ ein Poster zum Thema Schulsport anfertigen.

Ihr dürft in Teams zu zweit arbeiten. Eure Arbeit muss mit Computer geschrieben sein.
Das Poster soll farbig sein. Sprecht mit euren Sport- und Kunstlehrern über diesen Wettbewerb. Sie helfen euch sicherlich gerne weiter.
Eure Beiträge müssen bis 1. Juni bei unserem Fußballverein sein.

Preise:

- ★ Nehmen alle Schüler/Schülerinnen einer Klasse teil, so bekommt jeder ein kleines Geschenk.
- ★ Gewinne

1.–3. Preis	je ein Jahresticket für alle Fußballspiele unseres Vereins
4.–10. Preis	je zwei Eintrittskarten für ein Fußballspiel deiner Wahl
11.–20. Preis	je eine Eintrittskarte für ein Fußballspiel deiner Wahl

Wir freuen uns auf eure Beiträge und auf euch!!!
Eure Jugendabteilung des Fußballvereins FC 2020

Phil is an exchange student from Canada in your form. Your form is working on a contest and you're explaining the topic and the rules[1] to your friend from Canada.

☞ Wenn dir ein Wort auf Englisch nicht einfällt, versuche es zu umschreiben:
It's somebody who ... It's something that ... It's a place where ...

Phil I'm interested in your contest. Is it right that everybody must write a report about PE at your school?

You Well, you can write a report but you can do other things too.

Phil So, what are the other things? (4 things)

You ______________________________ (4P)

Phil That sounds interesting. Who can you interview then?

You ______________________________ (2P)

Phil And how are you going to send them the interview? (2 things)

You ______________________________ (2P)

Phil What is the first prize?

You ______________________________ (2P)

Phil Oh, I'd like to win a ticket like that. Who can work on the contest?

You ______________________________ (1P)

Phil I'd like to make a poster. What are the rules for the poster? (2 things)

You ______________________________ (2P)

Phil What about you? Could we work together?

You ______________________________ (1P)

Phil So, what are we waiting for? Let's go.

[1] rule [ru:l] *Regel, Vorschrift*

WRITING

Da dies eine zusätzliche Writing-Aufgabe ist, wird sie in der Gesamtpunktzahl für Klassenarbeit B nicht gewertet.

____/ 20

Now you want to write a report for the German contest together with Phil.
You have chosen the topic "A report about a sport event at your school".
Phil wants to send the report to his school magazine in Canada too so you're writing in English.

- Bei dieser Aufgabe hast du fast keine Vorgaben, so dass es sehr wichtig ist, dass du die drei Schritte beim Verfassen eines Textes beachtest. Siehe dazu den Hinweis zur Writing-Aufgabe auf S. 53 im Klassenarbeitstrainer.
- Schreibe deine Ideen unbedingt gleich auf Englisch auf, damit du später die notwendigen Wörter schon parat hast.
- Schreibe zunächst einen Entwurf und überprüfe ihn anhand der Checkliste in den Lösungen auf S. 34.
- Überarbeite dann deinen Entwurf solange, bis du ganz zufrieden bist.

SPEAKING

____/ 20

12 An interview for the contest[1]

Phil likes the idea of the contest so much that he is doing some interviews too. Listen to his interview with Kira.

New word
(to) come fifth *fünfter werden (bei einem Wettbewerb)*

13 Now you

Now Phil is interviewing Alexander, who is good at skiing. Imagine you are Alexander and are answering Phil's questions. Please make notes before you start with the interview. You can use the notepad below.

Höre dir zunächst Phils Fragen an und überlege mit Hilfe des Notizzettels, was du antworten kannst. Um hilfreiche Formulierungen zu finden, kannst du dir noch einmal das Interview mit Kira anhören.
Höre dir dann die Fragen ein zweites Mal an und beantworte sie. Halte den Text an, damit du genügend Zeit für deine Antworten hast.

Your notes:

1 **About myself**

– how old ____________________

– where from ____________________

– favourite sport *skiing*

– started with this sport when ____________________

2 **contests**

– local[2] contests: where/when ____________________

– all-German contests: where/when ____________________

3 **training**

– how often ____________________

– how long ____________________

[1] contest ['kɒntest] *Wettbewerb* [2] local ['ləʊkl] *Orts-, örtlich*

Klassenarbeit A

Gesamtpunktzahl ______ / 72 Note ______

READING

______ / 13

An article for TEEN MAGAZINE

1 STUDY SKILLS Skimming

______ / 1

Natalie L'Estane, one of the editors of TEEN MAGAZINE, has just got a new article for the fashion section. She skims the text to find out what it is about. Then she writes down one sentence about the article in her notes. Complete her sentence.

The article "My dream job: fashion designer" is about ______________________________

____

____

My dream job: fashion designer

Many things can help to get into a fashion school

by Simon Pey

Fashion designer – sounds like a dream job, eh? Well, it's my dream job, so I tried to get as much information as I could. I read many articles in books and magazines.
Last month I was able to talk to a British fashion designer who is a friend of my father's. So I got first-class information, if you know what I mean. And I thought it might be helpful for some of you too, so I want to share my information with you. Here is what I have found out so far:

There are quite a number of fashion schools in Great Britain. But the first thing you must know about them is that it's really difficult to get into one of them. You have to work really hard before a good fashion school will accept[1] you as a student. But here is the good news: if you really want to be a fashion designer and go to a fashion school there are things you can do. Here are some ideas for you:

1 Take a class in drawing at your school. It's best if you draw real people – if this is not possible, start drawing from photos of fashion models. Also learn about colours. You should know what colours look good together. Then draw your fashion ideas and keep your drawings in your portfolio[2] – you might need them later!

[1] accept [ək'sept] *hier: aufnehmen* [2] portfolio [pɔːt'fəʊliəʊ] *Mappe für Zeichnungen*

2 Learn to make clothes. First make clothes for yourself and then for your friends. Maybe your friends will even give you some money for the clothes – if they look good.

3 Find out about trendy fashion. Visit websites about fashion to see what colours are going to be the fashion. Think about what will be popular next year.

4 Learn about fashion in earlier centuries. Get to know old fashion styles likes those from the Victorian Age[1]. Have a look at clothes from the 1950s, 1960s, ... until today. Also find out about the important 20th-century designers like Chanel and Dior.

5 Learn how companies sell their fashion. What are the big department stores in your city? What shops sell the kind of fashion you are interested in? Find out about the customers[2] that buy these clothes. Who are they, how old are they, what job have they got, what do they do in their free time?

If you have more information or questions, just write an e-mail to: simon@pey.cim
I hope to hear from you soon.

2 Susan needs information

____ / 6

Susan (14) from Toronto wants to be a fashion designer. She has many questions.
When Susan reads the article "My dream job: fashion designer", she gets answers to ***six*** *of her questions.*
Tick (✔) these ***six*** *questions.*

1	Where are the really good fashion schools?	
2	What things can I do that will help me to get into a fashion school?	
3	Can I do something at my school?	
4	Do I need a lot of money to be a fashion designer?	
5	Will I need my own computer?	
6	How can I find out about the latest fashion?	
7	What can I put into my portfolio?	
8	Will I have to learn to make clothes?	
9	Will I easily find a job?	
10	Will I have to search the internet for information?	

[1] Victorian Age [vɪk'tɔːriən ˌeɪdʒ] *im Zeitalter von Königin Victoria (1837–1901)* [2] customer ['kʌstəmə] *Kunde, Kundin*

3 About Simon's article

____/6

Choose the answer that fits best.

1 Simon got his information from	a) magazines and his father.	
	b) books and the internet.	
	c) magazines and a fashion designer.	

2 It's not easy	a) to find a place in a fashion school.	
	b) to find out about the latest fashion.	
	c) to find information about a job as a fashion designer.	

3 In your portfolio you can put	a) the clothes you have made.	
	b) the latest fashion magazines.	
	c) your best fashion drawings.	

4 If you make clothes,	a) they must fit.	
	b) you should only make them for other people.	
	c) you might get some money.	

5 Find out about	a) fashion of different countries.	
	b) fashion of the past and today.	
	c) famous fashion labels.	

6 If you go to department stores,	a) study the customers there.	
	b) look around for good clothes.	
	c) find out about the companies that sell their clothes there.	

STUDY SKILLS

___/14

RESEARCH ON THE INTERNET Fashion Designers

*Susan wants to find the answers to some questions about 20th-century designers on the internet. What **key words** should she use in a search engine? Find the answers for her.*

1 What is the first name of the French designer Dior?

keywords: ______________________________

answer: ______________________________

2 Does Dior design clothes for men?

keywords: ______________________________

answer: ______________________________

3 When was Vivienne Westwood, the designer of the punk uniform, born?

keywords: ______________________________

answer: ______________________________

4 What is the name of the street in London where you can find the fashion house Chanel?

keywords: ______________________________

answer: ______________________________

5 Why did Karl Lagerfeld design a dress for Barbie?

keywords: ______________________________

answer: ______________________________

6 How much did the Levi Strauss Company pay for a 100-year-old pair of jeans in 1997 and why did they buy it?

keywords: ______________________________

answer: ______________________________

7 What is the name of fashion designer Stella McCartney's third baby?

keywords: ______________________________

answer: ______________________________

- Wenn du Schlüsselwörter, die zusammengehören (z. B. Vivienne Westwood) in Anführungszeichen setzt (▶ "Vivienne Westwood"), kommst du bei deiner Suche schneller zum Ziel.
- Wenn du nicht findest, was du suchst, füge weitere Schlüsselwörter hinzu oder versuche es mit neuen Schlüsselwörtern.

LANGUAGE

____ / 29

1 WORDS An alphabetical list

____ / 17

a) *The letters of the new words are mixed up. Put them in the correct order and write the words into the list. (9P)*

A	cracteuar	**N**	onte
B	**raphgyobi**	**O**	proae
C	earrce	**P**	eipp
D	efda	**Q**	tiqotkmuartnr
E	dretoi	**R**	erdidl
F	lofsk	**S**	escuscs
G		**T**	uent
H	dohhaeensp	**U**	
I	ulriarger	**V**	**noaatcvi**
J		**W**	ewka pu
K	peke	**X**	
L	reehlat	**Y**	
M	**chroeniomp**	**Z**	

b) *Think of **five** more new words that you have learned in Unit 5. Add them to the list. (5P)*

1 ______________________________

2 ______________________________

3 ______________________________

4 ______________________________

5 ______________________________

c) *Paraphrase the three words in **bold print** from **a)**. (3P)*

☞ Erkläre die Wörter mit einfachen englischen Sätzen.

1 ______________________________

2 ______________________________

3 ______________________________

2 GRAMMAR A holiday in Canada

______/6

Martin has been on holiday in Canada and is telling his classmates about some of the situations he was in. Write down what he says and use forms of ***be able to / be allowed to / have to*** *in the* ***simple past****.*

1

2

3

4

5

6

7

1 *We had to show our passports at the airport.*

2 At the tourist information we ______________________________.

3 We ______________________________ on the escalator[1].

4 The fortune-teller[2] ______________________________.

5 We ______________________________ at the museum.

6 The waitress[3] ______________________________.

7 We ______________________________ in the restaurant.

☞ (to) be able to = können
(to) be allowed to = dürfen
(to) have to = müssen

[1] escalator ['eskəleɪtə] *Rolltreppe* [2] fortune-teller ['fɔːtʃun telə] *Wahrsager/in* [3] waitress ['weɪtrəs] *Kellnerin, Bedienung*

3 GRAMMAR At the harbour in Toronto

_____ / 6

*Look at the picture and say what the people are doing or saying. Use **reflexive pronouns** or **each other**.*

1 Two little girls are pushing ______________________________.

2 A man is taking a picture of ______________________________.

3 Two old ladies are talking to ______________________________.

4 The twins are making ______________________________ sandwiches.

5 A dog has hurt ______________________________.

6 A boy: "I can see ______________________________ in the water!"

Reflexive pronouns (Reflexivpronomen)

I	myself	(ich) mir/mich	it	itself	(er/sie/es) sich
you	yourself	(du) dir/dich	we	ourselves	(wir) uns
he	himself	(er) sich	you	yourselves	(ihr) euch
she	herself	(sie) sich	they	themselves	(sie) sich

each other – themselves

sich = sich gegenseitig, einander ► **each other**
sich = sich selbst ► **themselves**

MEDIATION

____ / 16

> Beachte, dass du bei der Sprachmittlung einen Rollenwechsel vornehmen musst:
> Deine Mutter sagt z.B.: *„Frag sie, wie lange **sie** schon in Deutschland sind."*
> Sprichst du dann zu der anderen Person, wird aus dem **sie** im Deutschen ein **you** im Englischen: *How long have **you** been in Germany?*
> Das Gleiche gilt für dein Dolmetschen vom Englischen ins Deutsche.

A Canadian family in Germany

You are on a day trip with your parents near your hometown. You get to know a Canadian family. Because your parents don't speak very much English you help with the conversation.

Your mum Frag sie, wie lange sie schon in Deutschland sind und wie lange sie noch bleiben.

You ______________________________ (2P)

Woman We have been here for two weeks and we are staying until the end of the month.

You ______________________________ (2P)

Your mum Frag sie, wo sie hier wohnen.

You ______________________________ (1P)

Woman We are staying in a holiday apartment. It's small but we like it very much. It's good because we can cook our own meals. So we needn't go to a restaurant every day.

You ______________________________

____

______________________________ (3P)

Your mum Frag sie mal, ob sie noch Ideen für Ausflüge brauchen.

You ______________________________ (2P)

Woman Well, we have seen quite a lot of this area really. We want to visit one or two museums. Can you give us an idea where we could go?

You ______________________________

____

______________________________ (3P)

→

Your mum Wie wäre es, wenn wir die Familie in den nächsten Tagen zum Kaffee zu uns nach Hause einladen? Dann können wir ihre Pläne besprechen und werden etwas Gutes finden. Und ich backe einen guten deutschen Kuchen.

You ______________________________

____

______________________________ (3P)

Woman Thank you so much. We would like to come and of course we all like German cake.

Gesamtpunktzahl ohne Speaking ______ / 84 Note ______
Gesamtpunktzahl mit Speaking ______ / 99 Note ______

LISTENING

______ / 15

14 At Brandon's office[1]

Brandon, the main editor of TEEN MAGAZINE, is sitting in his office. A lot of people call him today. Listen to the telephone calls.

1 HEADLINES in the next TEEN MAGAZINE

______ / 7

Listen to the telephone calls. In the next TEEN MAGAZINE you will find **seven** *of these headlines. Tick (✔) them.*

1. 5 minutes that will keep you fit ☐
2. Susan – queen of girls' football ☐
3. Latest films at Toronto cinemas ☐
4. When did YOU last go to the cinema? ☐
5. My visit to a cinema in New York ☐
6. A report about Maths at school ☐
7. A first-class concert 50 students sing ☐
8. A report about my favourite singer ☐
9. An interview with a pilot ☐
10. Power learning ☐
11. Great fashion show at high school ☐
12. THIS YEAR AT THE BEACH ☐
13. 101 socks ☐

[1] office ['ɒfɪs] *Büro*

2 About the calls

_____ /8

***a)** Listen again to each of the telephone calls. Tick (✔) the correct box. (4P)*

First call

1 Mitsu is not sure about Paul's article	a) because she doesn't know Paul.	
	b) because Paul has written about a very old film.	
	c) because you can't see the film in Canada.	
	d) because she already has many articles.	

Second call

2 Jeff	a) wants to talk about a concert.	
	b) wants to talk to Robert.	
	c) is a friend of Brandon.	
	d) wants to call again on Friday.	

Third call

3 Lisa	a) calls because she wants to open a new section for TEEN MAGAZINE.	
	b) says she is a successful learner.	
	c) asks if she can come to Brandon's office.	
	d) hasn't got time this week.	

Fourth call

4 Natalie	a) talks about the best beaches.	
	b) is quite happy about the articles in her section.	
	c) doesn't have enough articles.	
	d) has already sent her material to Brandon.	

***b)** Listen again to all four telephone calls. Tick (✔) the **four** correct sentences. (4P)*

Brandon	1) thinks the new magazine will be good.	
	2) thinks Paul's article is boring.	
	3) knows the Chinese film Paul has seen.	
	4) doesn't know Robert's telephone number.	
	5) likes Lisa's idea.	
	6) will meet Lisa tomorrow.	
	7) rings up Natalie.	
	8) wants Natalie's material by tomorrow.	

LANGUAGE

____ / 37

1 WORDS An article in TEEN MAGAZINE

____ / 13

This is an article for the music section in the latest TEEN MAGAZINE. Fill in the missing words. There are four more words in the box than you need.

career • monitor • company • be sold out • sign • editor • headphones • biography • opera • study • release • success • vacation • stereo • headlines

Becoming a star

Hi, my name is Michael Howell and I'm 15 years old. I'm quite a good singer and I can play the guitar well. When you ____________ singing, you always dream of a big ____________ at the ____________. Sometimes I can already see my name in the newspaper ____________: "Michael Howell – a story of ____________". So when I heard about an audition[1] for a new CD with songs from local teenagers I went there. I had to go to the ____________ of the CD ____________ first and tell them some facts about myself. That was for a short ____________. Then the big moment came: I went into the studio and sang two songs. The lyrics were in front of me on a big ____________ and I had to wear the biggest ____________ you can imagine. After that I had to ____________ some papers. They will tell me in a few days if one of my songs will be on the CD. They will ____________ the CD in summer. So keep your eyes open – I think it will ____________ soon.

2 Getting by in English

____ / 5

Write what you would say in English.

Was sagst du, ...

1 ... wenn du denkst, dass etwas keinen Sinn hatte?

____

2 ... wenn du sagen willst: „Das liegt bei dir."?

____

3 ... wenn du die Schuld nicht bei dir siehst?

____

4 ... wenn du fragen willst, wozu etwas gut sein soll?

____

5 ... wenn du ankündigen willst, dass du (spätestens) bis 10 Uhr zu Hause bist?

____

[1] audition [ɔːˈdɪʃn] *Casting/Vorsingen*

3 GRAMMAR Rules for teenagers

____/9

TEEN MAGAZINE has asked its teenage readers about their rules at home. Look what they found out and make sentences with ***be allowed to / not be allowed to / have to****. (6P)*

1

2

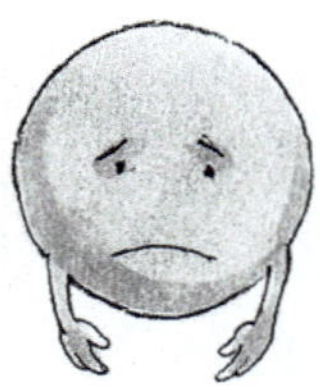

3

4

5

6

1 1 out of 5 teenagers ______________________________.

2 80 % of the teenagers ______________________________.

3 More than half the teenagers ______________________________.

4 Most teenagers ______________________________.

5 90 % of the teenagers ______________________________.

6 Almost all teenagers ______________________________.

Now you

What about your rules at home? Write three sentences and use ***be allowed to / not be allowed to*** *and* ***have to****. (3P)*

1 At home I ______________________________

2 ______________________________

3 ______________________________

4 GRAMMAR Always trouble with Mum

____ / 10

Look at the following e-mail that Jamie sent to TEEN MAGAZINE. He writes about his daily life and how his mum is making his life difficult for him.
Fill in the correct ***reflexive pronoun*** *or* ***each other*** *or* ***a dash (–)*** *if you don't need anything.*

Hello TEEN MAG,

Sometimes I really don't like my mum. She always tells me what to do and, more importantly, what not to do. She never lets me relax ____________. She always says I should prepare ____________ for my French tests. Well, she is so great!! She taught ____________ French when she was young. But I'm not interested in French. My friend and I are teaching ____________ to play the electric guitar! When my little brother and I fight with ____________ she tells us to stop, but it's so much fun and we have never hurt ____________. I only hurt ____________ once: I hit a door with my head when I ran away from him to hide ____________. In the mornings she keeps telling me that I must clean ____________ my teeth and get ____________ ready for school. I know that! I'm 14! I can look after ____________. I can remember ________ when my older sister was 14. Mum never said these things to her.

My mum and I are always shouting at ____________. Please help me!

Jamie

TEEN MAGAZINE's answer:

Dear Jamie,

Please calm ____________ down! All teenagers have problems with their mums, so don't worry ____________! It doesn't help if you argue ____________ with her all the time. Try to imagine ____________ what you would do if you had a teenage son. Maybe you and your mum should talk to ____________ and then you can tell her about your problems. I'm sure she will explain to you how she feels ____________ and maybe you can understand her.

TEEN MAG

WRITING

___ / 32

1 Correcting mistakes

___ / 12

Read the following text carefully and find the twelve mistakes. Then rewrite the text.

☞ Überprüfe den Text auf folgende Fehlerkategorien hin:
- Rechtschreibfehler (Groß-, Kleinschreibung, fehlende Buchstaben bei einem Wort, richtige Schreibweise bei der Pluralbildung: shelf – shelves; family – families)
- unregelmäßige Verbformen
- Zeiten (z.B. present perfect oder simple past)
- Präpositionen (falsch oder fehlend: I was angry ~~of~~ with (!) my friend)
- Wortstellung (im Englischen: subject – verb – object)
- Ist es das richtige Wort? (z.B.: Handy ≠ handy, sondern: mobile phone)

About my favourite star – a quiz

My favourite star is a man. He is born in england in 1982. When he was five years old he became his first guitar of his father. He has started to play and soon he was quite good. He learned to sing too. His friends liked his music. Very often asked they him to play on partys. When he was 18 he played his first concert and at the age of 22 released he his first CD. It was a sucess. It was selled over 500,000 time.

Can you guess who it is?

2 New editors for TEEN MAGAZINE

___ / 20

☞ In Unit 4 hast du dich intensiv mit kreativen Schreibaufgaben befasst. Auf S. 53 im Aufgabenteil und auf S. 34 in den Lösungen findest du Checklisten für vor und nach dem Schreiben eines Textes. Sieh dort noch einmal nach, worauf du achten musst, bevor du diese Aufgabe beginnst.

Dear readers of **TEEN MAGAZINE**,

We want to start new sections for **TEEN MAGAZINE** and are looking for motivated young editors. You'll find some ideas for a new section here:

cycling • quiz page • new games • computer world • Canada • holidays

Are you interested or have you got any other ideas?
If so, please send an e-mail to us: brandon@teenmagazine.cim

You want to start a new section for TEEN MAGAZINE.
Write an e-mail to Brandon with the following information:

- write about yourself and what you think about TEEN MAGAZINE
- write about the section you would like to open and say why you are interested in it (you may choose from the box or add a new idea)
- give details about your ideas for this section and about the first article you want to write (possible articles, ...)
- give your full name, address and phone number

Write about 150 words.

SPEAKING

____/15

15 Brandon's answering machine[1]

Brandon is the main editor of TEEN MAGAZINE. He can't be in his office this afternoon. So a lot of people leave a message for him on the answering machine. Listen to the messages.

Höre dir die Nachrichten ein zweites Mal an und notiere dir Formulierungen, die hilfreich sind, wenn du in **Now you** selbst eine Nachricht auf einem Anrufbeantworter hinterlässt.

Now you

Three more people leave their messages on the answering machine. Take their role. Give yourself a new name and a new telephone number for each part.

Das englische Alphabet zum Buchstabieren der Namen findest du in deinem Englischbuch auf S. 222.

First caller:
- gives her/his name and spells it
- has got an appointment on ... , but not possible
- says why
- asks for a call back for a new appointment
- suggests[2] a date for a new appointment
- gives her/his number

Second caller:
- gives her/his name and spells it
- says where and when she/he met Brandon
- has written an article about ...
- publish article?
- asks for a call back – gives her/his number

Third caller:
- gives her/his name
- has got more information about two young Germans who were in Montreal last month
- gives the name of one of them, spells the name and gives the telephone number
- tells a bit more about this person (what he is like, about his English, ...)
- says he is waiting for call

[1] answering machine ['ɑːnsərɪŋ məʃiːn] *Anrufbeantworter* [2] (to) suggest [sə'dʒest] *vorschlagen*

How to do well in a test

Countdown zum Testerfolg

Ein Test ist angekündigt? Kein Grund zur Panik. Wichtig ist, dass du weißt, worauf du dich vorbereiten musst. Im Zweifelsfall frag deine Lehrerin oder deinen Lehrer. Der Countdown kann beginnen!

Eine Woche vor dem Test

1 Lies noch einmal die **Texte** der zuletzt durchgenommenen Unit (A-Section und Text, eventuell auch das Background File). Fasse mündlich oder schriftlich zusammen, worum es ging.

2 Wiederhole den **Wortschatz** der Unit mit Hilfe des *Vocabulary* oder des *Wordmaster*.
Schreibe dir die Wörter und Wortverbindungen, die du immer wieder vergisst, auf ein Blatt Papier.
Eine Mindmap oder ein Wortfeld helfen beim Behalten.

3 Geh auch noch mal die neue **Grammatik** durch. Aufgaben zur Selbstüberprüfung und zum Üben findest du im *Practice*-Teil, auf der Seite „How am I doing?", im *Grammar File* (S. 172-189), in deinem *Workbook* und im *e-Workbook*.

Zwei Tage vor dem Test

1 Wiederhole den **Wortschatz**. Manche Wörter sitzen noch nicht? Schreibe einen kurzen Text, in dem du sie verwendest.

2 Lies die **Texte** ein weiteres Mal.

3 Erkläre einem Freund oder einer Freundin die neue **Grammatik**. Das klappt nicht richtig? Dann lies nochmal im *Grammar File* nach.

Am Abend vor dem Test

1 Entspanne dich. Du kannst lesen, dich in die Badewanne legen, Musik hören, fernsehen, ...

2 Geh zur gewohnten Zeit ins Bett.

Am Morgen des Tests

1 Steh rechtzeitig auf, damit du nicht hetzen musst.

2 Lies irgendetwas „zum Aufwärmen", aber schau nicht mehr in dein Schülerbuch.

Während des Tests

1 Denk daran: Du hast dich gut vorbereitet. Es gibt keinen Grund, nervös zu sein.

2 Konzentriere dich auf den Test, lass dich nicht ablenken.

3 Lies dir die Aufgaben genau durch. Dann löse zuerst die Aufgaben, die dir einfach scheinen. Wende dich erst danach den schwereren Aufgaben zu.

4 Aufgaben, die du bearbeitet hast, hakst du ab. So siehst du, wie du vorankommst, und behältst den Überblick.

5 Schau ab und zu auf die Uhr. Du solltest dir für den Schluss noch etwas Zeit einplanen, um deine Antworten noch einmal durchzulesen und wenn nötig zu korrigieren.

Aufgabenstellungen verstehen

Bevor du anfängst, die Aufgaben zu bearbeiten, vergewissere dich, dass du genau weißt, was du tun sollst. Lies die Aufgabe Wort für Wort langsam und gründlich und von Anfang bis Ende durch. Du kannst besonders wichtige Teile der Aufgabenstellung unterstreichen und die Aufgabe, wenn nötig, für dich in einzelne Schritte unterteilen.

Den folgenden Arbeitsanweisungen begegnest du häufig:

Add Verbinde eine Information oder einen Sachverhalt mit einer/einem anderen auf die geforderte Art und Weise.

Choose Wähle zwischen verschiedenen Möglichkeiten die passende Information aus.

Comment Kommentiere einen Sachverhalt durch die Darstellung deiner eigenen Meinung dazu. Begründe und erläutere sie möglichst genau.

Compare Vergleiche Dinge, Wörter oder Sachverhalte, indem du prüfst, ob und auf welche Weise sie gleiche oder verschiedene Eigenschaften, Aussehen, Bedeutungen oder Funktionen haben.

Complete Ergänze eine Information, indem du sie an dem dafür vorgesehenen Platz einträgst und damit z. B. einen Satz sinnvoll beendest.

Describe Beschreibe ein Objekt oder eine Person, d.h. stelle dar, wie sie aussehen, wie das Objekt funktioniert oder die Personen handeln. Vermeide eigene Wertungen wie z. B. „beautiful", „useful" oder „great".

Discuss Diskutiere ein Thema, eine Behauptung oder eine Aussage. Untersuche möglichst viele Seiten davon, z. B. Vor- und Nachteile, und stelle diese geordnet dar.

Explain Erkläre einen Sachverhalt, d. h. gib wesentliche Fakten über ihn und erläutere, wie sie logisch zusammenhängen.

Fill in Trage die geforderten Informationen in den dafür vorgesehenen Platz ein, z. B. in eine Lücke oder eine Tabelle.

List Schreibe einzelne oder mehrere Informationen übersichtlich und geordnet auf, z. B. in einer Reihe, Tabelle oder einem anderen Verzeichnis.

Listen Höre dir einen Text, einzelne Informationen oder Sachverhalte an.

Match Ordne die angegebenen Informationen einander zu, wie es die Aufgabe erfordert. Finde z. B. Satzanfänge und passende Satzenden und füge sie zusammen.

Use Verwende eine Tatsache, ein Wort usw. so, wie es in der Aufgabe gefordert wird.

Write a ... Schreibe etwas in einem geforderten Textformat auf, z. B. deinen Kommentar zu etwas oder eine Geschichte.